The Story of Geo§

Discovery

How the World Became Known

Joseph Jacobs

Alpha Editions

This edition published in 2024

ISBN : 9789362925039

Design and Setting By
Alpha Editions
www.alphaedis.com
Email - info@alphaedis.com

Contents

PREFACE

In attempting to get what is little less than a history of the world, from a special point of view, into a couple of hundred duodecimo pages, I have had to make three bites at my very big cherry. In the Appendix I have given in chronological order, and for the first time on such a scale in English, the chief voyages and explorations by which our knowledge of the world has been increased, and the chief works in which that knowledge has been recorded. In the body of the work I have then attempted to connect together these facts in their more general aspects. In particular I have grouped the great voyages of 1492-1521 round the search for the Spice Islands as a central motive. It is possible that in tracing the Portuguese and Spanish discoveries to the need of titillating the parched palates of the mediævals, who lived on salt meat during winter and salt fish during Lent, I may have unduly simplified the problem. But there can be no doubt of the paramount importance attached to the spices of the East in the earlier stages. The search for the El Dorado came afterwards, and is still urging men north to the Yukon, south to the Cape, and in a south-easterly direction to "Westralia."

Besides the general treatment in the text and the special details in the Appendix, I have also attempted to tell the story once more in a series of maps showing the gradual increase of men's knowledge of the globe. It would have been impossible to have included all these in a book of this size and price but for the complaisance of several publishing firms, who have given permission for the reproduction on a reduced scale of maps that have already been prepared for special purposes. I have specially to thank Messrs. Macmillan for the two dealing with the Portuguese discoveries, and derived from Mr. Payne's excellent little work on European Colonies; Messrs. Houghton, Mifflin, & Co., of Boston, for several illustrating the discovery of America, from Mr. J. Fiske's "School History of the United States;" and Messrs. Phillips for the arms of Del Cano, so clearly displaying the "spicy" motive of the first circumnavigation of the globe.

I have besides to thank the officials of the Royal Geographical Society, especially Mr. Scott Keltie and Dr. H. R. Mill, for the readiness with which they have placed the magnificent resources of the library and map-room of that national institution at my disposal, and the kindness with which they have answered my queries and indicated new sources of information.

J. J.

INTRODUCTION

How was the world discovered? That is to say, how did a certain set of men who lived round the Mediterranean Sea, and had acquired the art of recording what each generation had learned, become successively aware of the other parts of the globe? Every part of the earth, so far as we know, has been inhabited by man during the five or six thousand years in which Europeans have been storing up their knowledge, and all that time the inhabitants of each part, of course, were acquainted with that particular part: the Kamtschatkans knew Kamtschatka, the Greenlanders, Greenland; the various tribes of North American Indians knew, at any rate, that part of America over which they wandered, long before Columbus, as we say, "discovered" it.

Very often these savages not only know their own country, but can express their knowledge in maps of very remarkable accuracy. Cortes traversed over 1000 miles through Central America, guided only by a calico map of a local cacique. An Eskimo named Kalliherey drew out, from his own knowledge of the coast between Smith Channel and Cape York, a map of it, varying only in minute details from the Admiralty chart. A native of Tahiti, named Tupaia, drew out for Cook a map of the Pacific, extending over forty-five degrees of longitude (nearly 3000 miles), giving the relative size and position of the main islands over that huge tract of ocean. Almost all geographical discoveries by Europeans have, in like manner, been brought about by means of guides, who necessarily knew the country which their European masters wished to "discover."

What, therefore, we mean by the history of geographical discovery is the gradual bringing to the knowledge of the nations of civilisation surrounding the Mediterranean Sea the vast tracts of land extending in all directions from it. There are mainly two divisions of this history—the discovery of the Old World and that of the New, including Australia under the latter term. Though we speak of geographical discovery, it is really the discovery of new tribes of men that we are thinking of. It is only quite recently that men have sought for knowledge about lands, apart from the men who inhabit them. One might almost say that the history of geographical discovery, properly so called, begins with Captain Cook, the motive of whose voyages was purely scientific curiosity. But before his time men wanted to know one another for two chief reasons: they wanted to conquer, or they wanted to trade; or perhaps we could reduce the motives to one—they wanted to conquer, because they wanted to trade. In our own day we have seen a remarkable mixture of all three motives, resulting in the

European partition of Africa—perhaps the most remarkable event of the latter end of the nineteenth century. Speke and Burton, Livingstone and Stanley, investigated the interior from love of adventure and of knowledge; then came the great chartered trading companies; and, finally, the governments to which these belong have assumed responsibility for the territories thus made known to the civilised world. Within forty years the map of Africa, which was practically a blank in the interior, and, as will be shown, was better known in 1680 than in 1850, has been filled up almost completely by researches due to motives of conquest, of trade, or of scientific curiosity.

In its earlier stages, then, the history of geographical discovery is mainly a history of conquest, and what we shall have to do will be to give a short history of the ancient world, from the point of view of how that world became known. "Became known to whom?" you may ask; and we must determine that question first. We might, of course, take the earliest geographical work known to us—the tenth chapter of Genesis—and work out how the rest of the world became known to the Israelites when they became part of the Roman Empire; but in history all roads lead to Rome or away from it, and it is more useful for every purpose to take Rome as our centre-point. Yet Rome only came in as the heir of earlier empires that spread the knowledge of the earth and man by conquest long before Rome was of importance; and even when the Romans were the masters of all this vast inheritance, they had not themselves the ability to record the geographical knowledge thus acquired, and it is to a Greek named Ptolemy, a professor of the great university of Alexandria, to whom we owe our knowledge of how much the ancient world knew of the earth. It will be convenient to determine this first, and afterwards to sketch rapidly the course of historical events which led to the knowledge which Ptolemy records.

In the Middle Ages, much of this knowledge, like all other, was lost, and we shall have to record how knowledge was replaced by imagination and theory. The true inheritors of Greek science during that period were the Arabs, and the few additions to real geographical knowledge at that time were due to them, except in so far as commercial travellers and pilgrims brought a more intimate knowledge of Asia to the West.

The discovery of America forms the beginning of a new period, both in modern history and in modern geography. In the four hundred years that have elapsed since then, more than twice as much of the inhabited globe has become known to civilised man than in the preceding four thousand years. The result is that, except for a few patches of Africa, South America, and round the Poles, man knows roughly what are the physical resources of the world he inhabits, and, except for minor details, the history of geographical discovery is practically at an end.

Besides its interest as a record of war and adventure, this history gives the successive stages by which modern men have been made what they are. The longest known countries and peoples have, on the whole, had the deepest influence in the forming of the civilised character. Nor is the practical utility of this study less important. The way in which the world has been discovered determines now-a-days the world's history. The great problems of the twentieth century will have immediate relation to the discoveries of America, of Africa, and of Australia. In all these problems, Englishmen will have most to say and to do, and the history of geographical discovery is, therefore, of immediate and immense interest to Englishmen.

[*Authorities:* Cooley, *History of Maritime and Inland Discoveries*, 3 vols., 1831; Vivien de Saint Martin, *Histoire de la Géographie*, 1873.]

CHAPTER I

THE WORLD AS KNOWN TO THE ANCIENTS

Before telling how the ancients got to know that part of the world with which they finally became acquainted when the Roman Empire was at its greatest extent, it is as well to get some idea of the successive stages of their knowledge, leaving for the next chapter the story of how that knowledge was obtained. As in most branches of organised knowledge, it is to the Greeks that we owe our acquaintance with ancient views of this subject. In the early stages they possibly learned something from the Phœnicians, who were the great traders and sailors of antiquity, and who coasted along the Mediterranean, ventured through the Straits of Gibraltar, and traded with the British Isles, which they visited for the tin found in Cornwall. It is even said that one of their admirals, at the command of Necho, king of Egypt, circumnavigated Africa, for Herodotus reports that on the homeward voyage the sun set in the sea on the right hand. But the Phœnicians kept their geographical knowledge to themselves as a trade secret, and the Greeks learned but little from them.

The first glimpse that we have of the notions which the Greeks possessed of the shape and the inhabitants of the earth is afforded by the poems passing under the name of HOMER. These poems show an intimate knowledge of Northern Greece and of the western coasts of Asia Minor, some acquaintance with Egypt, Cyprus, and Sicily; but all the rest, even of the Eastern Mediterranean, is only vaguely conceived by their author. Where he does not know he imagines, and some of his imaginings have had a most important influence upon the progress of geographical knowledge. Thus he conceives of the world as being a sort of flat shield, with an extremely wide river surrounding it, known as Ocean. The centre of this shield was at Delphi, which was regarded as the "navel" of the inhabited world. According to Hesiod, who is but little later than Homer, up in the far north were placed a people known as the *Hyperboreani*, or those who dwelt at the back of the north wind; whilst a corresponding place in the south was taken by the Abyssinians. All these four conceptions had an important influence upon the views that men had of the world up to times comparatively recent. Homer also mentioned the pigmies as living in Africa. These were regarded as fabulous, till they were re-discovered by Dr. Schweinfurth and Mr. Stanley in our own time.

It is probably from the Babylonians that the Greeks obtained the idea of an all-encircling ocean. Inhabitants of Mesopotamia would find themselves reaching the ocean in almost any direction in which they travelled, either the Caspian, the Black Sea, the Mediterranean, or the Persian Gulf. Accordingly, the oldest map of the world which has been found is one accompanying a cuneiform inscription, and representing the plain of Mesopotamia with the Euphrates flowing through it, and the whole surrounded by two concentric circles, which are named briny waters. Outside these, however, are seven detached islets, possibly representing the seven zones or climates into which the world was divided according to the ideas of the Babylonians, though afterwards they resorted to the ordinary four cardinal points. What was roughly true of Babylonia did not in any way answer to the geographical position of Greece, and it is therefore probable that in the first place they obtained their ideas of the surrounding ocean from the Babylonians.

THE EARLIEST MAP OF THE WORLD

It was after the period of Homer and Hesiod that the first great expansion of Greek knowledge about the world began, through the extensive colonisation which was carried on by the Greeks around the Eastern Mediterranean. Even to this day the natives of the southern part of Italy speak a Greek dialect, owing to the wide extent of Greek colonies in that country, which used to be called "Magna Grecia," or "Great Greece." Marseilles also one of the Greek colonies (600 B.C.), which, in its turn, sent out other colonies along the Gulf of Lyons. In the East, too, Greek cities were dotted along the coast of the Black Sea, one of which, Byzantium, was destined to be of world-historic importance. So, too, in North Africa, and among the islands of the Ægean Sea, the Greeks colonised throughout the sixth and fifth centuries B.C., and in almost every case communication was kept up between the colonies and the mother-country.

Now, the one quality which has made the Greeks so distinguished in the world's history was their curiosity; and it was natural that they should desire to know, and to put on record, the large amount of information brought to the mainland of Greece from the innumerable Greek colonies. But to record geographical knowledge, the first thing that is necessary is a map, and accordingly it is a Greek philosopher named ANAXIMANDER of Miletus, of the sixth century B.C., to whom we owe the invention of map-drawing. Now, in order to make a map of one's own country, little astronomical knowledge is required. As we have seen, savages are able to draw such maps; but when it comes to describing the relative positions of countries divided from one another by seas, the problem is not so easy. An Athenian would know roughly that Byzantium (now called Constantinople) was somewhat to the east and to the north of him, because in sailing thither he would have to sail towards the rising sun, and would find the climate getting colder as he approached Byzantium. So, too, he might roughly guess that Marseilles was somewhere to the west and north of him; but how was he to fix the relative position of Marseilles and Byzantium to one another? Was Marseilles more northerly than Byzantium? Was it very far away from that city? For though it took longer to get to Marseilles, the voyage was winding, and might possibly bring the vessel comparatively near to Byzantium, though there might be no direct road between the two cities. There was one rough way of determining how far north a place stood: the very slightest observation of the starry heavens would show a traveller that as he moved towards the north, the pole-star rose higher up in the heavens. How much higher, could be determined by the angle formed by a stick pointing to the pole-star, in relation to one held horizontally. If, instead of two sticks, we cut out a piece of metal or wood to fill up the enclosed angle, we get the earliest form of the sun-dial, known as the *gnomon*, and according to the shape of the gnomon the latitude of a place is determined. Accordingly, it is not surprising to find that the invention of the gnomon is also attributed to Anaximander, for without some such instrument it would have been impossible for him to have made any map worthy of the name. But it is probable that Anaximander did not so much invent as introduce the gnomon, and, indeed, Herodotus, expressly states that this instrument was derived from the Babylonians, who were the earliest astronomers, so far as we know. A curious point confirms this, for the measurement of angles is by degrees, and degrees are divided into sixty seconds, just as minutes are. Now this division into sixty is certainly derived from Babylonia in the case of time measurement, and is therefore of the same origin as regards the measurement of angles.

We have no longer any copy of this first map of the world drawn up by Anaximander, but there is little doubt that it formed the foundation of a similar map drawn by a fellow-townsman of Anaximander, HECATÆUS of Miletus, who seems to have written the first formal geography. Only fragments of this are extant, but from them we are able to see that it was of the nature of a *periplus*, or seaman's guide, telling how many days' sail it was from one point to another, and in what direction. We know also that he arranged his whole subject into two books, dealing respectively with Europe and Asia, under which latter term he included part of what we now know as Africa. From the fragments scholars have been able to reproduce the rough outlines of the map of the world as it presented itself to Hecatæus. From this it can be seen that the Homeric conception of the surrounding ocean formed a chief determining feature in Hecatæus's map. For the rest, he was acquainted with the Mediterranean, Red, and Black Seas, and with the great rivers Danube, Nile, Euphrates, Tigris, and Indus.

The next great name in the history of Greek geography is that of HERODOTUS of Halicarnassus, who might indeed be equally well called the Father of Geography as the Father of History. He travelled much in Egypt, Babylonia, Persia, and on the shores of the Black Sea, while he was acquainted with Greece, and passed the latter years of his life in South Italy. On all these countries he gave his fellow-citizens accurate and tolerably full information, and he had diligently collected knowledge about countries in their neighbourhood. In particular he gives full details of Scythia (or Southern Russia), and of the satrapies and royal roads of Persia. As a rule, his information is as accurate as could be expected at such an early date, and he rarely tells marvellous stories, or if he does, he points out himself their untrustworthiness. Almost the only traveller's yarn which Herodotus reports without due scepticism is that of the ants of India that were bigger than foxes and burrowed out gold dust for their ant-hills.

One of the stories he relates is of interest, as seeming to show an anticipation of one of Mr. Stanley's journeys. Five young men of the Nasamonians started from Southern Libya, W. of the Soudan, and journeyed for many days west till they came to a grove of trees, when they were seized by a number of men of very small stature, and conducted through marshes to a great city of black men of the same size, through which a large river flowed. This Herodotus identifies with the Nile, but, from the indication of the journey given by him, it would seem more probable that it was the Niger, and that the Nasamonians had visited Timbuctoo! Owing to this statement of Herodotus, it was for long thought that the Upper Nile flowed east and west.

After Herodotus, the date of whose history may be fixed at the easily remembered number of 444 B.C., a large increase of knowledge was obtained of the western part of Asia by the two expeditions of Xenophon and of Alexander, which brought the familiar knowledge of the Greeks as far as India. But besides these military expeditions we have still extant several log-books of mariners, which might have added considerably to Greek geography. One of these tells the tale of an expedition of the Carthaginian admiral named Hanno, down the western coast of Africa, as far as Sierra Leone, a voyage which was not afterwards undertaken for sixteen hundred years. Hanno brought back from this voyage hairy skins, which, he stated, belonged to men and women whom he had captured, and who were known to the natives by the name of Gorillas. Another log-book is that of a Greek named Scylax, who gives the sailing distances between nearly all ports on the Mediterranean and Black Seas, and the number of days required to pass from one to another. From this it would seem that a Greek merchant vessel could manage on the average fifty miles a day. Besides this, one of Alexander's admirals, named Nearchus, learned to carry his ships from the mouth of the Indus to the Arabian Gulf. Later on, a Greek sailor, Hippalus, found out that by using the monsoons at the appropriate times, he could sail direct from Arabia to India without laboriously coasting along the shores of Persia and Beluchistan, and in consequence the Greeks gave his name to the monsoon. For information about India itself, the Greeks were, for a long time, dependent upon the account of Megasthenes, an ambassador sent by Seleucus, one of Alexander's generals, to the Indian king of the Punjab.

While knowledge was thus gained of the East, additional information was obtained about the north of Europe by the travels of one PYTHEAS, a native of Marseilles, who flourished about the time of Alexander the Great (333 B.C.), and he is especially interesting to us as having been the first civilised person who can be identified as having visited Britain. He seems to have coasted along the Bay of Biscay, to have spent some time in England,—which he reckoned as 40,000 stadia (4000 miles) in circumference,—and he appears also to have coasted along Belgium and Holland, as far as the mouth of the Elbe. Pytheas is, however, chiefly known in the history of geography as having referred to the island of Thule, which he described as the most northerly point of the inhabited earth, beyond which the sea became thickened, and of a jelly-like consistency. He does not profess to have visited Thule, and his account probably refers to the existence of drift ice near the Shetlands.

All this new information was gathered together, and made accessible to the Greek reading world, by ERATOSTHENES, librarian of Alexandria (240-196 B.C.), who was practically the founder of scientific geography. He was the first to attempt any accurate measurement of the size of the earth, and of its inhabited portion. By his time the scientific men of Greece had become quite aware of the fact that the earth was a globe, though they considered that it was fixed in space at the centre of the universe. Guesses had even been made at the size of this globe, Aristotle fixing its circumference at 400,000 stadia (or 40,000 miles), but Eratosthenes attempted a more accurate measurement. He compared the length of the shadow thrown by the sun at Alexandria and at Syene, near the first cataract of the Nile, which he assumed to be on the same meridian of longitude, and to be at about 5000 stadia (500 miles) distance. From the difference in the length of the shadows he deduced that this distance represented one-fiftieth of the circumference of the earth, which would accordingly be about 250,000 stadia, or 25,000 geographical miles. As the actual circumference is 24,899 English miles, this was a very near approximation, considering the rough means Eratosthenes had at his disposal.

Having thus estimated the size of the earth, Eratosthenes then went on to determine the size of that portion which the ancients considered to be habitable. North and south of the lands known to him, Eratosthenes and all the ancients considered to be either too cold or too hot to be habitable; this portion he reckoned to extend to 38,000 stadia, or 3800 miles. In reckoning the extent of the habitable portion from east to west, Eratosthenes came to the conclusion that from the Straits of Gibraltar to the east of India was about 80,000 stadia, or, roughly speaking, one-third of the earth's surface. The remaining two-thirds were supposed to be covered by the ocean, and Eratosthenes prophetically remarked that "if it were not that the vast extent of the Atlantic Sea rendered it impossible, one might almost sail from the coast of Spain to that of India along the same parallel." Sixteen hundred years later, as we shall see, Columbus tried to carry out this idea. Eratosthenes based his calculations on two fundamental lines, corresponding in a way to our equator and meridian of Greenwich: the first stretched, according to him, from Cape St. Vincent, through the Straits of Messina and the island of Rhodes, to Issus (Gulf of Iskanderun); for his starting-line in reckoning north and south he used a meridian passing through the First Cataract, Alexandria, Rhodes, and Byzantium.

The next two hundred years after Eratosthenes' death was filled up by the spread of the Roman Empire, by the taking over by the Romans of the vast possessions previously held by Alexander and his successors and by the Carthaginians, and by their spread into Gaul, Britain, and Germany. Much of the increased knowledge thus obtained was summed up in the geographical work of STRABO, who wrote in Greek about 20 B.C. He introduced from the extra knowledge thus obtained many modifications of the system of Eratosthenes, but, on the whole, kept to his general conception of the world. He rejected, however, the existence of Thule, and thus made the world narrower; while he recognised the existence of Ierne, or Ireland; which he regarded as the most northerly part of the habitable world, lying, as he thought, north of Britain.

Between the time of Strabo and that of Ptolemy, who sums up all the knowledge of the ancients about the habitable earth, there was only one considerable addition to men's acquaintance with their neighbours, contained in a seaman's manual for the navigation of the Indian Ocean, known as the *Periplus* of the Erythræan Sea. This gave very full and tolerably accurate accounts of the coasts from Aden to the mouth of the Ganges, though it regarded Ceylon as much greater, and more to the south, than it really is; but it also contains an account of the more easterly parts of Asia, Indo-China, and China itself, "where the silk comes from." This had an important influence on the views of Ptolemy, as we shall see, and indirectly helped long afterwards to the discovery of America.

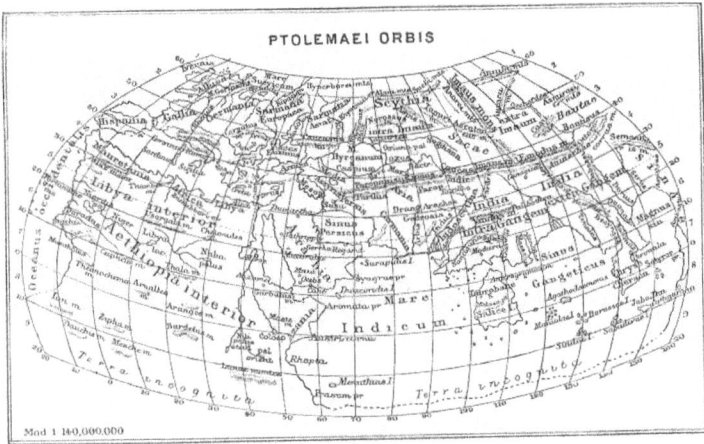

PTOLEMAEI ORBIS

It was left to PTOLEMY of Alexandria to sum up for the ancient world all the knowledge that had been accumulating from the time of Eratosthenes to his own day, which we may fix at about 150 A.D. He took all the information he could find in the writings of the preceding four hundred years, and reduced it all to one uniform scale; for it is to him that we owe the invention of the method and the names of latitude and longitude. Previous writers had been content to say that the distance between one point and another was so many stadia, but he reduced all this rough reckoning to so many degrees of latitude and longitude, from fixed lines as starting-points. But, unfortunately, all these reckonings were rough calculations, which are almost invariably beyond the truth; and Ptolemy, though the greatest of ancient astronomers, still further distorted his results by assuming that a degree was 500 stadia, or 50 geographical miles. Thus when he found in any of his authorities that the distance between one port and another was 500 stadia, he assumed, in the first place, that this was accurate, and, in the second, that the distance between the two places was equal to a degree of latitude or longitude, as the case might be. Accordingly he arrived at the result that the breadth of the habitable globe was, as he put it, twelve hours of longitude (corresponding to 180°)—nearly one-third as much again as the real dimensions from Spain to China. The consequence of this was that the distance from Spain to China *westward* was correspondingly diminished by sixty degrees (or nearly 4000 miles), and it was this error that ultimately encouraged Columbus to attempt his epoch-making voyage.

Ptolemy's errors of calculation would not have been so extensive but that he adopted a method of measurement which made them accumulative. If he had chosen Alexandria for the point of departure in measuring longitude, the errors he made when reckoning westward would have been counterbalanced by those reckoning eastward, and would not have resulted in any serious distortion of the truth; but instead of this, he adopted as his point of departure the Fortunatæ Insulæ, or Canary Islands, and every degree measured to the east of these was one-fifth too great, since he assumed that it was only fifty miles in length. I may mention that so great has been the influence of Ptolemy on geography, that, up to the middle of the last century, Ferro, in the Canary Islands, was still retained as the zero-point of the meridians of longitude.

Another point in which Ptolemy's system strongly influenced modern opinion was his departure from the previous assumption that the world was surrounded by the ocean, derived from Homer. Instead of Africa being thus cut through the middle by the ocean, Ptolemy assumed, possibly from vague traditional knowledge, that Africa extended an unknown length to the south, and joined on to an equally unknown continent far to the east, which, in the Latinised versions of his astronomical work, was termed "terra australis incognita," or "the unknown south land." As, by his error with regard to the breadth of the earth, Ptolemy led to Columbus; so, by his mistaken notions as to the "great south land," he prepared the way for the discoveries of Captain Cook. But notwithstanding these errors, which were due partly to the roughness of the materials which he had to deal with, and partly to scientific caution, Ptolemy's work is one of the great monuments of human industry and knowledge. For the Old World it remained the basis of all geographical knowledge up to the beginning of the last century, just as his astronomical work was only finally abolished by the work of Newton. Ptolemy has thus the rare distinction of being the greatest authority on two important departments of human knowledge—astronomy and geography—for over fifteen hundred years. Into the details of his description of the world it is unnecessary to go. The map will indicate how near he came to the main outlines of the Mediterranean, of Northwest Europe, of Arabia, and of the Black Sea. Beyond these regions he could only depend upon the rough indications and guesses of untutored merchants. But it is worth while referring to his method of determining latitude, as it was followed up by most succeeding geographers. Between the equator and the most northerly point known to him, he divides up the earth into horizontal strips, called by him "climates," and determined by the average length of the longest day in each. This is a very rough method of determining latitude, but it was probably, in most cases, all that Ptolemy had to depend upon, since the measurement of angles would be a rare accomplishment even in modern times, and would only exist among a few mathematicians and astronomers in Ptolemy's days. With him the history of geographical knowledge and discovery in the ancient world closes.

In this chapter I have roughly given the names and exploits of the Greek men of science, who summed up in a series of systematic records the knowledge obtained by merchants, by soldiers, and by travellers of the extent of the world known to the ancients. Of this knowledge, by far the largest amount was gained, not by systematic investigation for the purpose of geography, but by military expeditions for the purpose of conquest. We must now retrace our steps, and give a rough review of the various stages of conquest. We must now retrace our steps, and give a rough review of the various stages of conquest by which the different regions of the Old World became known to the Greeks and the Roman Empire, whose knowledge Ptolemy summarises.

[*Authorities:* Bunbury, *History of Ancient Geography,* 2 vols., 1879; Tozer, *History of Ancient Geography,* 1897.]

CHAPTER II

THE SPREAD OF CONQUEST IN THE ANCIENT WORLD

In a companion volume of this series, "The Story of Extinct Civilisations in the East," will be found an account of the rise and development of the various nations who held sway over the west of Asia at the dawn of history. Modern discoveries of remarkable interest have enabled us to learn the condition of men in Asia Minor as early as 4000 B.C. All these early civilisations existed on the banks of great rivers, which rendered the land fertile through which they passed.

We first find man conscious of himself, and putting his knowledge on record, along the banks of the great rivers Nile, Euphrates, and Tigris, Ganges and Yang-tse-Kiang. But for our purposes we are not concerned with these very early stages of history. The Egyptians got to know something of the nations that surrounded them, and so did the Assyrians. A summary of similar knowledge is contained in the list of tribes given in the tenth chapter of Genesis, which divides all mankind, as then known to the Hebrews, into descendants of Shem, Ham, and Japhet— corresponding, roughly, to Asia, Europe, and Africa. But in order to ascertain how the Romans obtained the mass of information which was summarised for them by Ptolemy in his great work, we have merely to concentrate our attention on the remarkable process of continuous expansion which ultimately led to the existence of the Roman Empire.

All early histories of kingdoms are practically of the same type. A certain tract of country is divided up among a certain number of tribes speaking a common language, and each of these tribes ruled by a separate chieftain. One of these tribes then becomes predominant over the rest, through the skill in war or diplomacy of one of its chiefs, and the whole of the tract of country is thus organised into one kingdom. Thus the history of England relates how the kingdom of Wessex grew into predominance over the whole of the country; that of France tells how the kings who ruled over the Isle of France spread their rule over the rest of the land; the history of Israel is mainly an account of how the tribe of Judah obtained the hegemony of the rest of the tribes; and Roman history, as its name implies, informs us how the inhabitants of a single city grew to be the masters of the whole known world. But their empire had been prepared for them by a long series of similar expansions, which might be described as the successive swallowing up of empire after empire, each becoming overgrown in the process, till at last the series was concluded by the Romans swallowing up the whole. It was this gradual spread of dominion which, at each stage, increased men's knowledge of surrounding nations, and it therefore comes within our province to roughly sum up these stages, as part of the story of geographical discovery.

Regarded from the point of view of geography, this spread of man's knowledge might be compared to the growth of a huge oyster-shell, and, from that point of view, we have to take the north of the Persian Gulf as the apex of the shell, and begin with the Babylonian Empire. We first have the kingdom of Babylon—which, in the early stages, might be best termed Chaldæa—in the south of Mesopotamia (or the valley between the two rivers, Tigris and Euphrates), which, during the third and second millennia before our era, spread along the valley of the Tigris. But in the fourteenth century B.C., the Assyrians to the north of it, though previously dependent upon Babylon, conquered it, and, after various vicissitudes, established themselves throughout the whole of Mesopotamia and much of the surrounding lands. In 604 B.C. the capital of this great empire was moved once more to Babylon, so that in the last stage, as well as in the first, it may be called Babylonia. For purposes of distinction, however, it will be as well to call these three successive stages Chaldæa, Assyria, and Babylonia.

Meanwhile, immediately to the east, a somewhat similar process had been gone through, though here the development was from north to south, the Medes of the north developing a powerful empire in the north of Persia, which ultimately fell into the hands of Cyrus the Great in 546 B.C. He then proceeded to conquer the kingdom of Lydia, in the northwest part of Asia Minor, which had previously inherited the dominions of the Hittites. Finally he proceeded to seize the empire of Babylonia, by his successful attack on the capital, 538 B.C. He extended his rule nearly as far as India on one side, and, as we know from the Bible, to the borders of Egypt on the other. His son Cambyses even succeeded in adding Egypt for a time to the Persian Empire. The oyster-shell of history had accordingly expanded to include almost the whole of Western Asia.

The next two centuries are taken up in universal history by the magnificent struggle of the Greeks against the Persian Empire—the most decisive conflict in all history, for it determined whether Europe or Asia should conquer the world. Hitherto the course of conquest had been from east to west, and if Xerxes' invasion had been successful, there is little doubt that the westward tendency would have continued. But the larger the tract of country which an empire covers—especially when different tribes and nations are included in it—the weaker and less organised it becomes. Within little more than a century of the death of Cyrus the Great the Greeks discovered the vulnerable point in the Persian Empire, owing to an expedition of ten thousand Greek mercenaries under Xenophon, who had been engaged by Cyrus the younger in an attempt to capture the Persian

Empire from his brother. Cyrus was slain, 401 B.C., but the ten thousand, under the leadership of Xenophon, were enabled, to hold their own against all the attempts of the Persians to destroy them, and found their way back to Greece.

Meanwhile the usual process had been going on in Greece by which a country becomes consolidated. From time to time one of the tribes into which that mountainous country was divided obtained supremacy over the rest: at first the Athenians, owing to the prominent part they had taken in repelling the Persians; then the Spartans, and finally the Thebans. But on the northern frontiers a race of hardy mountaineers, the Macedonians, had consolidated their power, and, under Philip of Macedon, became masters of all Greece. Philip had learned the lesson taught by the successful retreat of the ten thousand, and, just before his death, was preparing to attack the Great King (of Persia) with all the forces which his supremacy in Greece put at his disposal. His son Alexander the Great carried out Philip's intentions. Within twelve years (334-323 B.C.) he had conquered Persia, Parthia, India (in the strict sense, *i.e.* the valley of the Indus), and Egypt. After his death his huge empire was divided up among his generals, but, except in the extreme east, the whole of it was administered on Greek methods. A Greek-speaking person could pass from one end to the other without difficulty, and we can understand how a knowledge of the whole tract of country between the Adriatic and the Indus could be obtained by Greek scholars. Alexander founded a large number of cities, all bearing his name, at various points of his itinerary; but of these the most important was that at the mouth of the Nile, known to this day as Alexandria. Here was the intellectual centre of the whole Hellenic world, and accordingly it was here, as we have seen, that Eratosthenes first wrote down in a systematic manner all the knowledge about the habitable earth which had been gained mainly by Alexander's conquests.

Important as was the triumphant march of Alexander through Western Asia, both in history and in geography, it cannot be said to have added so very much to geographical knowledge, for Herodotus was roughly acquainted with most of the country thus traversed, except towards the east of Persia and the north-west of India. But the itineraries of Alexander and his generals must have contributed more exact knowledge of the distances between the various important centres of population, and enabled Eratosthenes and his successors to give them a definite position on their maps of the world. What they chiefly learned from Alexander and his immediate successors was a more accurate knowledge of North-West India. Even as late as Strabo, the sole knowledge possessed at Alexandria of Indian places was that given by Megasthenes, the ambassador to India in the third century B.C.

Meanwhile, in the western portion of the civilised world a similar process had gone on. In the Italian peninsula the usual struggle had gone on between the various tribes inhabiting it. The fertile plain of Lombardy was not in those days regarded as belonging to Italy, but was known as Cisalpine Gaul. The south of Italy, as we have seen, was mainly inhabited by Greek colonists, and was called Great Greece. Between these tracts of country the Italian territory was inhabited by three sets of federate tribes— the Etrurians, the Samnites, and the Latins. During the 230 years between 510 B.C. and 280 B.C. Rome was occupied in obtaining the supremacy among these three sets of tribes, and by the latter date may be regarded as having consolidated Central Italy into an Italian federation, centralised at Rome. At the latter date, the Greek king Pyrrhus of Epirus, attempted to arouse the Greek colonies in Southern Italy against the growing power of Rome; but his interference only resulted in extending the Roman dominion down to the heel and big toe of Italy.

If Rome was to advance farther, Sicily would be the next step, and just at that moment Sicily was being threatened by the other great power of the West—Carthage. Carthage was the most important of the colonies founded by the Phœnicians (probably in the ninth century B.C.), and pursued in the Western Mediterranean the policy of establishing trading stations along the coast, which had distinguished the Phœnicians from their first appearance in history. They seized all the islands in that division of the sea, or at any rate prevented any other nation from settling in Corsica, Sardinia, and the Balearic Isles. In particular Carthage took possession of the western part of Sicily, which had been settled by sister Phœnician colonies. While Rome did everything in its power to consolidate its conquests by admitting the other Italians to some share in the central government, Carthage only regarded its foreign possessions as so many openings for trade. In fact, it dealt with the western littoral of the Mediterranean something like the East India Company treated the coast of Hindostan: it established factories at convenient spots. But just as the East India Company found it necessary to conquer the neighbouring territory in order to secure peaceful trade, so Carthage extended its conquests all down the western coast of Africa and the south-east part of Spain, while Rome was extending into Italy. To continue our conchological analogy, by the time of the first Punic War Rome and Carthage had each expanded into a shell, and between the two intervened the eastern section of the island of Sicily. As the result of this, Rome became master of Sicily, and then the final struggle took place with Hannibal in the second Punic War, which resulted in Rome becoming possessed of Spain and Carthage. By the year 200 B.C. Rome was practically master of the Western Mediterranean, though it took another century to consolidate its heritage from Carthage in Spain and Mauritania. During that century—the second before our era—Rome also extended its

Italian boundaries to the Alps by the conquest of Cisalpine Gaul, which, however, was considered outside Italy, from which it was separated by the river Rubicon. In that same century the Romans had begun to interfere in the affairs of Greece, which easily fell into their hands, and thus prepared the way for their inheritance of Alexander's empire.

This, in the main, was the work of the first century before our era, when the expansion of Rome became practically concluded. This was mainly the work of two men, Cæsar and Pompey. Following the example of his uncle, Marius, Cæsar extended the Roman dominions beyond the Alps to Gaul, Western Germany, and Britain; but from our present standpoint it was Pompey who prepared the way for Rome to carry on the succession of empire in the more civilised portions of the world, and thereby merited his title of "Great." He pounded up, as it were, the various states into which Asia Minor was divided, and thus prepared the way for Roman dominion over Western Asia and Egypt. By the time of Ptolemy the empire was thoroughly consolidated, and his map and geographical notices are only tolerably accurate within the confines of the empire.

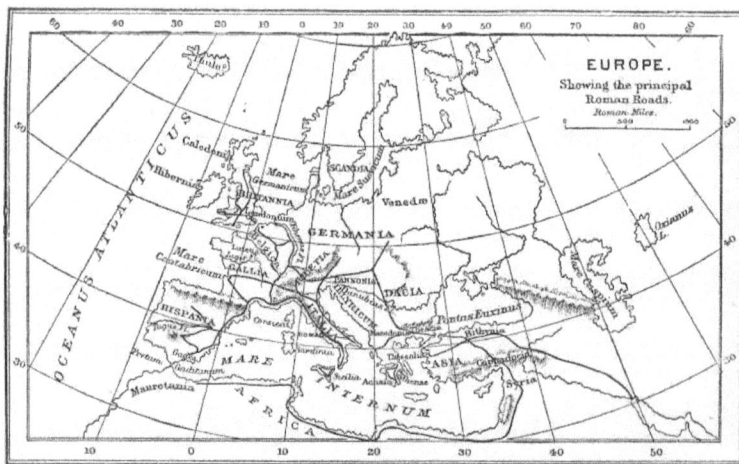

EUROPE.
Showing the principal Roman Roads.

One of the means by which the Romans were enabled to consolidate their dominion must be here shortly referred to. In order that their legions might easily pass from one portion of this huge empire to another, they built roads, generally in straight lines, and so solidly constructed that in many places throughout Europe they can be traced even to the present day, after the lapse of fifteen hundred years. Owing to them, in a large measure, Rome was enabled to preserve its empire intact for nearly five hundred years, and even to this day one can trace a difference in the civilisation of those countries over which Rome once ruled, except where the devastating influence of Islam has passed like a sponge over the old Roman provinces. Civilisation, or the art of living together in society, is practically the result of Roman law, and this sense all roads in history lead to Rome.

The work of Claudius Ptolemy sums up to us the knowledge that the Romans had gained by their inheritance, on the western side, of the Carthaginian empire, and, on the eastern, of the remains of Alexander's empire, to which must be added the conquests of Cæsar in North-West Europe. Cæsar is, indeed, the connecting link between the two shells that had been growing throughout ancient history. He added Gaul, Germany, and Britain to geographical knowledge, and, by his struggle with Pompey, connected the Levant with his northerly conquests. One result of his imperial work must be here referred to. By bringing all civilised men under one rule, he prepared them for the worship of one God. This was not without its influence on travel and geographical discovery, for the great barrier between mankind had always been the difference of religion, and Rome, by breaking down the exclusiveness of local religions, and substituting for them a general worship of the majesty of the Emperor, enabled all the inhabitants of this vast empire to feel a certain communion with one another, which ultimately, as we know, took on a religious form.

The Roman Empire will henceforth form the centre from which to regard any additions to geographical knowledge. As we shall see, part of the knowledge acquired by the Romans was lost in the Dark Ages succeeding the break-up of the empire; but for our purposes this may be neglected and geographical discovery in the succeeding chapters may be roughly taken to be additions and corrections of the knowledge summed up by Claudius Ptolemy.

CHAPTER III

GEOGRAPHY IN THE DARK AGES

We have seen how, by a slow process of conquest and expansion, the ancient world got to know a large part of the Eastern Hemisphere, and how this knowledge was summed up in the great work of Claudius Ptolemy. We have now to learn how much of this knowledge was lost or perverted—how geography, for a time, lost the character of a science, and became once more the subject of mythical fancies similar to those which we found in its earliest stages. Instead of knowledge which, if not quite exact, was at any rate approximately measured, the mediæval teachers who concerned themselves with the configuration of the inhabited world substituted their own ideas of what ought to be.[1] This is a process which applies not alone to geography, but to all branches of knowledge, which, after the fall of the Roman Empire, ceased to expand or progress, became mixed up with fanciful notions, and only recovered when a knowledge of ancient science and thought was restored in the fifteenth century. But in geography we can more easily see than in other sciences the exact nature of the disturbing influence which prevented the acquisition of new knowledge.

[Footnote 1: It is fair to add that Professor Miller's researches have shown that some of the "unscientific" qualities of the mediæval *mappæ mundi* were due to Roman models.]

Briefly put, that disturbing influence was religion, or rather theology; not, of course, religion in the proper sense of the word, or theology based on critical principles, but theological conceptions deduced from a slavish adherence to texts of Scripture, very often seriously misunderstood. To quote a single example: when it is said in Ezekiel v. S, "This is Jerusalem: I have set it in the midst of the nations... round about her," this was not taken by the mediæval monks, who were the chief geographers of the period, as a poetical statement, but as an exact mathematical law, which determined the form which all mediæval maps took. Roughly speaking, of course, there was a certain amount of truth in the statement, since Jerusalem would be about the centre of the world as known to the ancients—at least, measured from east to west; but, at the same time, the mediæval geographers adopted the old Homeric idea of the ocean surrounding the habitable world, though at times there was a tendency to keep more closely to the words of Scripture about the four corners of the earth. Still, as a rule, the orthodox conception of the world was that of a circle enclosing a sort of T square, the east being placed at the top, Jerusalem in the centre; the Mediterranean Sea naturally divided the lower half of the circle, while the Ægean and Red Seas were regarded as spreading out right and left perpendicularly, thus dividing the top part of the world, or Asia, from the lower part, divided equally between Europe on the left and Africa on the right. The size of the Mediterranean Sea, it will be seen, thus determined the dimensions of the three continents. One of the chief errors to which this led was to cut off the whole of the south of Africa, which rendered it seemingly a short voyage round that continent on the way to India. As we shall see, this error had important and favourable results on geographical discovery.

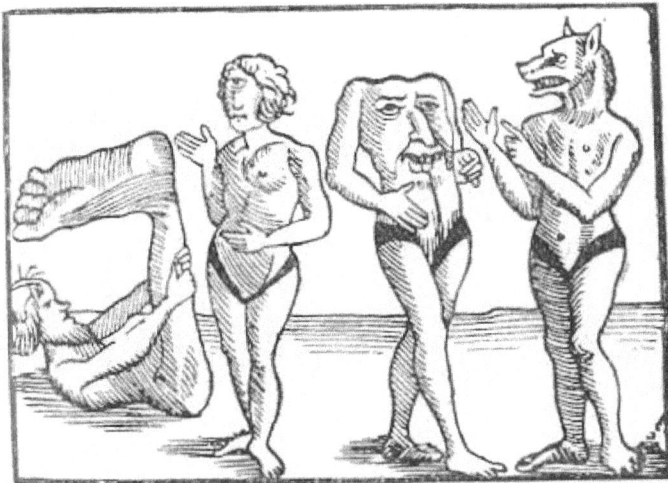

GEOGRAPHICAL MONSTERS

Another result of this conception of the world as a T within an O, was to expand Asia to an enormous extent; and as this was a part of the world which was less known to the monkish map-makers of the Middle Ages, they were obliged to fill out their ignorance by their imagination. Hence they located in Asia all the legends which they had derived either from Biblical or classical sources. Thus there was a conception, for which very little basis is to be found in the Bible, of two fierce nations named Gog and Magog, who would one day bring about the destruction of the civilised world. These were located in what would have been Siberia, and it was thought that Alexander the Great had penned them in behind the Iron Mountains. When the great Tartar invasion came in the thirteenth century, it was natural to suppose that these were no less than the Gog and Magog of legend. So, too, the position of Paradise was fixed in the extreme east, or, in other words, at the top of mediæval maps. Then, again, some of the classical authorities, as Pliny and Solinus, had admitted into their geographical accounts legends of strange tribes of monstrous men, strangely different from normal humanity. Among these may be mentioned the Sciapodes, or men whose feet were so large that when it was hot they could rest on their backs and lie in the shade. There is a dim remembrance of these monstrosities in Shakespeare's reference to

"The Anthropophagi, and men whose heads
Do grow beneath their shoulders."

In the mythical travels of Sir John Maundeville there are illustrations of these curious beings, one of which is here reproduced. Other tracts of country were supposed to be inhabited by equally monstrous animals. Illustrations of most of these were utilised to fill up the many vacant spaces in the mediæval maps of Asia.

One author, indeed, in his theological zeal, went much further in modifying the conceptions of the habitable world. A Christian merchant named Cosmas, who had journeyed to India, and was accordingly known as COSMAS INDICOPLEUSTES, wrote, about 540 A.D., a work entitled "Christian Topography," to confound what he thought to be the erroneous views of Pagan authorities about the configuration of the world. What especially roused his ire was the conception of the spherical form of the earth, and of the Antipodes, or men who could stand upside down. He drew a picture of a round ball, with four men standing upon it, with their feet on opposite sides, and asked triumphantly how it was possible that all four could stand upright? In answer to those who asked him to explain how he could account for day and night if the sun did not go round the earth, he supposed that there was a huge mountain in the extreme north, round which the sun moved once in every twenty-four hours. Night was when the sun was going round the other side of the mountain. He also proved, entirely to his own satisfaction, that the sun, instead of being greater, was very much smaller than the earth. The earth was, according to him, a moderately sized plane, the inhabited parts of which were separated from the antediluvian world by the ocean, and at the four corners of the whole were the pillars which supported the heavens, so that the whole universe was something like a big glass exhibition case, on the top of which was the firmament, dividing the waters above and below it, according to the first chapter of Genesis.

THE HEREFORD MAP.

Cosmas' views, however interesting and amusing they are, were too extreme to gain much credence or attention even from the mediæval monks, and we find no reference to them in the various *mappæ mundi* which sum up their knowledge, or rather ignorance, about the world. One of the most remarkable of these maps exists in England at Hereford, and the plan of it given on p. 53 will convey as much information as to early mediæval geography as the ordinary reader will require. In the extreme east, *i.e.* at the top, is represented the Terrestrial Paradise; in the centre is Jerusalem; beneath this, the Mediterranean extends to the lower edge of the map, with its islands very carefully particularised. Much attention is given to the rivers throughout, but very little to the mountains. The only real increase of actual knowledge represented in the map is that of the north-east of Europe, which had I naturally become better known by the invasion of the Norsemen. But how little real knowledge was possessed of this portion of Europe is proved by the fact that the mapmaker placed near Norway the Cynocephali, or dog-headed men, probably derived from some confused accounts of Indian monkeys. Near them are placed the Gryphons, "men most wicked, for among their misdeeds they also make garments for themselves and their horses out of the skins of their enemies." Here, too, is placed the home of the Seven Sleepers, who lived for ever as a standing miracle to convert the heathen. The shape given to the British Islands will be observed as due to the necessity of keeping the circular form of the inhabited world. Other details about England we may leave for the present.

It is obvious that maps such as the Hereford one would be of no practical utility to travellers who desired to pass from one country to another; indeed, they were not intended for any such purpose. Geography had ceased to be in any sense a practical science; it only ministered to men's sense of wonder, and men studied it mainly in order to learn about the marvels of the world. When William of Wykeham drew up his rules for the Fellows and Scholars of New College, Oxford, he directed them in the long winter evenings to occupy themselves with "singing, or reciting poetry, or with the chronicles of the different kingdoms, or with the *wonders of the world.*" Hence almost all mediæval maps are filled up with pictures of these wonders, which were the more necessary as so few people could read. A curious survival of this custom lasted on in map-drawing almost to the beginning of this century, when the spare places in the ocean were adorned with pictures of sailing ships or spouting sea monsters.

When men desired to travel, they did not use such maps as these, but rather itineraries, or road-books, which did not profess to give the shape of the countries through which a traveller would pass, but only indicated the chief towns on the most-frequented roads. This information was really derived from classical times, for the Roman emperors from time to time directed such road-books to be drawn up, and there still remains an almost complete itinerary of the Empire, known as the Peutinger Table, from the name of the German merchant who first drew the attention of the learned world to it. A condensed reproduction is given on the following page, from which it will be seen that no attempt is made to give anything more than the roads and towns. Unfortunately, the first section of the table, which started from Britain, has been mutilated, and we only get the Kentish coast. These itineraries were specially useful, as the chief journeys of men were in the nature of pilgrimages; but these often included a sort of commercial travelling, pilgrims often combining business and religion on their journeys. The chief information about Eastern Europe which reached the West was given by the succession of pilgrims who visited Palestine up to the time of the Crusades. Our chief knowledge of the geography of Europe daring the five centuries between 500 and 1000 A.D. is given in the reports of successive pilgrims.

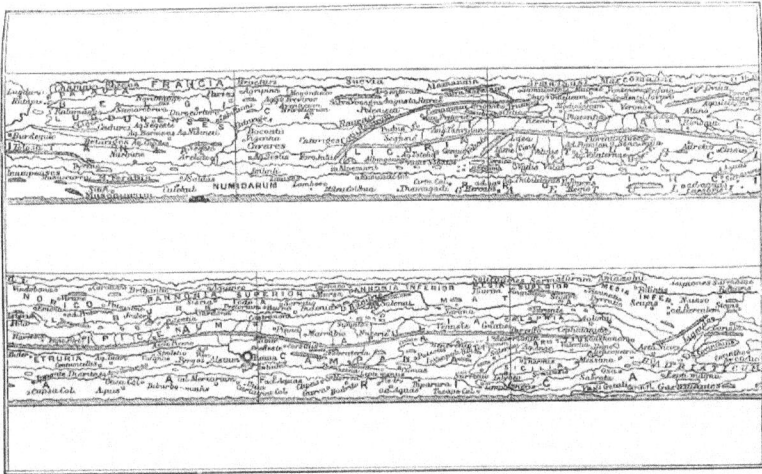

THE PEUTINGER TABLE—WESTERN PART.

This period may be regarded as the Dark Age of geographical knowledge, during which wild conceptions like those contained in the Hereford map were substituted for the more accurate measurements of the ancients. Curiously enough, almost down to the time of Columbus the learned kept to these conceptions, instead of modifying them by the extra knowledge gained during the second period of the Middle Ages, when travellers of all kinds obtained much fuller information of Asia, North Europe, and even, as, we shall see, of some parts of America.

It is not altogether surprising that this period should have been so backward in geographical knowledge, since the map of Europe itself, in its political divisions, was entirely readjusted during this period. The thousand years of history which elapsed between 450 and 1450 were practically taken up by successive waves of invasion from the centre of Asia, which almost entirely broke up the older divisions of the world.

In the fifth century three wandering tribes, invaded the Empire, from the banks of the Vistula, the Dnieper, and the Volga respectively. The Huns came from the Volga, in the extreme east, and under Attila, "the Hammer of God," wrought consternation in the Empire; the Visigoths, from the Dnieper, attacked the Eastern Empire; while the Vandals, from the Vistula, took a triumphant course through Gaul and Spain, and founded for a time a Vandal empire in North Africa. One of the consequences of this movement was to drive several of the German tribes into France, Italy, and Spain, and even over into Britain; for it is from this stage in the world's history that we can trace the beginning of England, properly so called, just as the invasion of Gaul by the Franks at this time means the beginning of French history. By the eighth century the kingdom of the Franks extended all over France, and included most of Central Germany; while on Christmas Day, 800, Charles the Great was crowned at Rome, by the Pope, Emperor of the Holy Roman Empire, which professed to revive the glories of the old empire, but made a division between the temporal power held by the Emperor and the spiritual power held by the Pope.

One of the divisions of the Frankish Empire deserves attention, because upon its fate rested the destinies of most of the nations of Western Europe. The kingdom of Burgundy, the buffer state between France and Germany, has now entirely disappeared, except as the name of a wine; but having no natural boundaries, it was disputed between France and Germany for a long period, and it may be fairly said that the Franco-Prussian War was the last stage in its history up to the present. A similar state existed in the east of Europe, viz. the kingdom of Poland, which was equally indefinite in shape, and has equally formed a subject of dispute between the nations of Eastern Europe. This, as is well known, only disappeared as an independent state in 1795, when it finally ceased to act as a buffer between Russia and the rest of Europe. Roughly speaking, after the settlement of the Germanic tribes within the confines of the Empire, the history of Europe, and therefore its historical geography, may be summed up as a struggle for the possession of Burgundy and Poland.

But there was an important interlude in the south-west of Europe, which must engage our attention as a symptom of a world-historic change in the condition of civilisation. During the course of the seventh and eighth centuries (roughly, between 622 and 750) the inhabitants of the Arabian peninsula burst the seclusion which they had held since the beginning, almost, of history, and, inspired by the zeal of the newly-founded religion of Islam, spread their influence from India to Spain, along the southern littoral of the Mediterranean. When they had once settled down, they began to recover the remnants of Græco-Roman science that had been lost on the north shores of the Mediterranean. The Christians of Syria used Greek for their sacred language, and accordingly when the Sultans of Bagdad desired to know something of the wisdom of the Greeks, they got Syriac-speaking Christians to translate some of the scientific works of the Greeks, first into Syriac, and thence into Arabic. In this way they obtained a knowledge of the great works of Ptolemy, both in astronomy—which they regarded as the more important, and therefore the greatest, Almagest—and also in geography, though one can easily understand the great modifications which the strange names of Ptolemy must have undergone in being transcribed, first into Syriac and then into Arabic. We shall see later on some of the results of the Arabic Ptolemy.

The conquests of the Arabs affected the knowledge of geography in a twofold way: by bringing about the Crusades, and by renewing the acquaintance of the west with the east of Asia. The Arabs were acquainted with South-Eastern Africa as far south as Zanzibar and Sofala, though, following the views of Ptolemy as to the Great Unknown South Land, they imagined that these spread out into the Indian Ocean towards India. They seem even to have had some vague knowledge of the sources of the Nile. They were also acquainted with Ceylon, Java, and Sumatra, and they were the first people to learn the various uses to which the cocoa-nut can be put. Their merchants, too, visited China as early as the ninth century, and we have from their accounts some of the earliest descriptions of the Chinese, who were described by them as a handsome people, superior in beauty to the Indians, with fine dark hair, regular features, and very like the Arabs. We shall see later on how comparatively easy it was for a Mohammedan to travel from one end of the known world to the other, owing to the community of religion throughout such a vast area.

Some words should perhaps be said on the geographical works of the Arabs. One of the most important of these, by Yacut, is in the form of a huge Gazetteer, arranged in alphabetical order; but the greatest geographical work of the Arabs is by EDRISI, geographer to King Roger of Sicily, 1154, who describes the world somewhat after the manner of Ptolemy, but with modifications of some interest. He divides the world into seven horizontal strips, known as "climates," and ranging from the equator to the British Isles. These strips are subdivided into eleven sections, so that the world, in Edrisi's conception, is like a chess-board, divided into seventy-seven squares, and his work consists of an elaborate description of each of these squares taken one by one, each climate being worked through regularly, so that you might get parts of France in the

THE WORLD ACCORDING TO IBN HAUKAL.

eighth and ninth squares, and other parts in the sixteenth and seventeenth. Such a method was not adapted to give a clear conception of separate countries, but this was scarcely Edrisi's object. When the Arabs—or, indeed, any of the ancient or mediæval writers—wanted wanted to describe a land, they wrote about the tribe or nation inhabiting it, and not about the position of the towns in it; in other words, they drew a marked distinction between ethnology and geography.

But the geography of the Arabs had little or no influence upon that of Europe, which, so far as maps went, continued to be based on fancy instead of fact almost up to the time of Columbus.

Meanwhile another movement had been going on during the eighth and ninth centuries, which helped to make Europe what it is, and extended considerably the common knowledge of the northern European peoples. For the first time since the disappearance of the Phœnicians, a great naval power came into existence in Norway, and within a couple of centuries it had influenced almost the whole sea-coast of Europe. The Vikings, or Sea-Rovers, who kept their long ships in the *viks*, or fjords, of Norway, made vigorous attacks all along the coast of Europe, and in several cases formed stable governments, and so made, in a way, a sort of crust for Europe, preventing any further shaking of its human contents. In Iceland, in England, in Ireland, in Normandy, in Sicily, and at Constantinople (where they formed the *Varangi*, or body-guard of the Emperor), as well as in Russia, and for a time in the Holy Land, Vikings or Normans founded kingdoms between which there was a lively interchange of visits and knowledge.

They certainly extended their voyages to Greenland, and there is a good deal of evidence for believing that they travelled from Greenland to Labrador and Newfoundland. In the year 1001, an Icelander named Biorn, sailing to Greenland to visit his father, was driven to the south-west, and came to a country which they called Vinland, inhabited by dwarfs, and having a shortest day of eight hours, which would correspond roughly to 50° north latitude. The Norsemen settled there, and as late as 1121 the Bishop of Greenland visited them, in order to convert them to Christianity. There is little reason to doubt that this Vinland was on the mainland of North America, and the Norsemen were therefore the first Europeans to discover America. As late as 1380, two Venetians, named Zeno, visited Iceland, and reported that there was a tradition there of a land named Estotiland, a thousand miles west of the Faroe Islands, and south of Greenland. The people were reported to be civilised and good seamen, though unacquainted with the use of the compass, while south of them were savage cannibals, and still more to the south-west another civilised people, who built large cities and temples, but offered up human victims in them. There seems to be here a dim knowledge of the Mexicans.

The great difficulty in maritime discovery, both for the ancients and the men of the Middle Ages, was the necessity of keeping close to the shore. It is true they might guide themselves by the sun during the day, and by the pole-star at night, but if once the sky was overcast, they would become entirely at a loss for their bearings. Hence the discovery of the polar tendency of the magnetic needle was a necessary prelude to any extended voyages away from land. This appears to have been known to the Chinese from quite ancient times, and utilised on their junks as early as the eleventh century. The Arabs, who voyaged to Ceylon and Java, appear to have learnt its use from the Chinese, and it is probably from them that the mariners of Barcelona first introduced its use into Europe. The first mention of it is given in a treatise on Natural History by Alexander Neckam, foster-brother of Richard, Cœur de Lion. Another reference, in a satirical poem of the troubadour, Guyot of Provence (1190), states that mariners can steer to the north star without seeing it, by following the direction of a needle floating in a straw in a basin of water, after it had been touched by a magnet. But little use, however, seems to have been made of this, for Brunetto Latini, Dante's tutor, when on a visit to Roger Bacon in 1258, states that the friar had shown him the magnet and its properties, but adds that, however useful the discovery, "no master mariner would dare to use it, lest he should be thought to be a magician." Indeed, in the form in which it was first used it would be of little practical utility, and it was not till the method was found of balancing it on a pivot and fixing it on a card, as at present used, that it became a necessary part of a sailor's outfit. This practical improvement is attributed to one Flavio Gioja, of Amalfi, in the beginning of the fourteenth century.

THE MEDITERRANEAN COAST IN THE PORTULANI.

When once the mariner's compass had come into general use, and its indications observed by master mariners in their voyages, a much more practical method was at hand for determining the relative positions of the different lands. Hitherto geographers (*i.e.*, mainly the Greeks and Arabs) had had to depend for fixing relative positions on the vague statements in the itineraries of merchants and soldiers; but now, with the aid of the compass, it was not difficult to determine the relative position of one point to another, while all the windings of a road could be fixed down on paper without much difficulty. Consequently, while the learned monks were content with the mixture of myth and fable which we have seen to have formed the basis of their maps of the world, the seamen of the Mediterranean were gradually building up charts of that sea and the neighbouring lands which varied but little from the true position. A chart of this kind was called a Portulano, as giving information of the best routes from port to port, and Baron Nordenskiold has recently shown how all these *portulani* are derived from a single Catalan map which has been lost, but must have been compiled between 1266 and 1291. And yet there were some of the learned who were not above taking instruction from the practical knowledge of the seamen. In 1339, one Angelico Dulcert, of Majorca, made an elaborate map of the world on the principle of the portulano, giving the coast line—at least of the Mediterranean—with remarkable accuracy. A little later, in 1375, a Jew of the same island, named Cresquez, made an improvement on this by introducing into the eastern parts of the map the recently acquired knowledge of Cathay, or China, due to the great traveller Marco Polo. His map (generally known as the Catalan Map, from the language of the inscriptions plentifully scattered over it) is divided into eight horizontal strips, and on the preceding page will be found a reduced reproduction, showing how very accurately the coast line of the Mediterranean was reproduced in these portulanos.

With the portulanos, geographical knowledge once more came back to the lines of progress, by reverting to the representation of fact, and, by giving an accurate representation of the coast line, enabled mariners to adventure more fearlessly and to return more safely, while they gave the means for recording any further knowledge. As we shall see, they aided Prince Henry the Navigator to start that series of geographical investigation which led to the discoveries that close the Middle Ages. With them we may fairly close the history of mediæval geography, so far as it professed to be a systematic branch of knowledge.

We must now turn back and briefly sum up the additions to knowledge made by travellers, pilgrims, and merchants, and recorded in literary shape in the form of travels.

[*Authorities:* Lelewel, *Géographie du Moyen Age*, 4 vols. and atlas, 1852; C. R. Beazley, *Dawn of Geography*, 1897, and Introduction to *Prince Henry the Navigator*, 1895; Nordenskiold, *Periplus*, 1897.]

CHAPTER IV

MEDIÆVAL TRAVELS

In the Middle Ages—that is, in the thousand years between the irruption of the barbarians into the Roman Empire in the fifth century and the discovery of the New World in the fifteenth—the chief stages of history which affect the extension of men's knowledge of the world were: the voyages of the Vikings in the eighth and ninth centuries, to which we have already referred; the Crusades, in the twelfth and thirteenth centuries; and the growth of the Mongol Empire in the thirteenth and fourteenth centuries. The extra knowledge obtained by the Vikings did not penetrate to the rest of Europe; that brought by the Crusades, and their predecessors, the many pilgrimages to the Holy Land, only restored to Western Europe the knowledge already stored up in classical antiquity; but the effect of the extension of the Mongol Empire was of more wide-reaching importance, and resulted in the addition of knowledge about Eastern Asia which was not possessed by the Romans, and has only been surpassed in modern times during the present century.

Towards the beginning of the thirteenth century, Chinchiz Khan, leader of a small Tatar tribe, conquered most of Central and Eastern Asia, including China. Under his son, Okkodai, these Mongol Tatars turned from China to the West, conquered Armenia, and one of the Mongol generals, named Batu, ravaged South Russia and Poland, and captured Buda-Pest, 1241. It seemed as if the prophesied end of the world had come, and the mighty nations Gog and Magog had at last burst forth to fulfil the prophetic words. But Okkodai died suddenly, and these armies were recalled. Universal terror seized Europe, and the Pope, as the head of Christendom, determined to send ambassadors to the Great Khan, to ascertain his real intentions. He sent a friar named John of Planocarpini, from Lyons, in 1245, to the camp of Batu (on the Volga), who passed him on to the court of the Great Khan at Karakorum, the capital of his empire, of which only the slightest trace is now left on the left bank of the Orkhon, some hundred miles south of Lake Baikal.

Here, for the first time, they heard of a kingdom on the east coast of Asia which was not yet conquered by the Mongols, and which was known by the name of Cathay. Fuller information was obtained by another friar, named WILLIAM RUYSBROEK, or Rubruquis, a Fleming, who also visited Karakorum as an ambassador from St. Louis, and got back to Europe in 1255, and communicated some of his information to Roger Bacon. He says: "These Cathayans are little fellows, speaking much through the nose, and, as is general with all those Eastern people, their eyes are very narrow.... The common money of Cathay consists of pieces of cotton paper; about a palm in length and breadth, upon which certain lines are printed, resembling the seal of Mangou Khan. They do their writing with a pencil such as painters paint with, and a single character of theirs comprehends several letters, so as to form a whole word." He also identifies these Cathayans with the Seres of the ancients. Ptolemy knew of these as possessing the land where the silk comes from, but he had also heard of the Sinæ, and failed to identify the two. It has been conjectured that the name of China came to the West by the sea voyage, and is a Malay modification, while the names Seres and Cathayans came overland, and thus caused confusion.

Other Franciscans followed these, and one of them, John of Montecorvino, settled at Khanbalig (imperial city), or Pekin, as Archbishop (ob. 1358); while Friar Odoric of Pordenone, near Friuli, travelled in India and China between 1316 and 1330, and brought back an account of his voyage, filled with most marvellous mendacities, most of which were taken over bodily into the work attributed to Sir John Maundeville.

The information brought back by these wandering friars fades, however, into insignificance before the extensive and accurate knowledge of almost the whole of Eastern Asia brought back to Europe by Marco Polo, a Venetian, who spent eighteen years of his life in the East. His travels form an epoch in the history of geographical discovery only second to the voyages of Columbus.

In 1260, two of his uncles, named Nicolo and Maffeo Polo, started from Constaninople on a trading venture to the Crimea, after which they were led to visit Bokhara, and thence on to the court of the Great Khan, Kublai, who received them very graciously, and being impressed with the desirability of introducing Western civilisation into the new Mongolian empire, he entrusted them with a message to the Pope, demanding one hundred wise men of the West to teach the Mongolians the Christian religion and Western arts. The two brothers returned to their native place, Venice, in 1269, but found no Pope to comply with the Great Khan's request; for Clement IV. had died the year before, and his successor had not yet been appointed. They waited about for a couple of years till Gregory X. was elected, but he only meagrely responded to the Great Khan's demands, and instructed two Dominicans to accompany the Polos, who on this occasion took with them their young nephew Marco, a lad of seventeen. They started in November 1271, but soon lost the company of the Dominicans, who lost heart and went back.

They went first to Ormuz, at the mouth of the Persian Gulf, then struck northward through Khorasan Balkh to the Oxus, and thence on to the Plateau of Pomir. Thence they passed the Great Desert of Gobi, and at last reached Kublai in May 1275, at his summer residence in Kaipingfu. Notwithstanding that they had not carried out his request, the Khan received them in a friendly manner, and was especially taken by Marco, whom he took into his own service; and quite recently a record has been found in the Chinese annals, stating that in the year 1277 a certain Polo was nominated a Second-Class Commissioner of the PrivyCouncil. His duty was to travel on various missions to Eastern Tibet, to Cochin China, and even to India. The Polos amassed much wealth owing to the Khan's favour, but found him very unwilling to let them return to Europe. Marco Polo held several important posts; for three years he was Governor of the great city of Yanchau, and it seemed likely that he would die in the service of Kublai Khan.

But, owing to a fortunate chance, they were at last enabled to get back to Europe. The Khan of Persia desired to marry a princess of the Great Khan's family, to whom he was related, and as the young lady upon whom the choice fell could not be expected to undergo the hardships of the overland journey from China to Persia, it was decided to send her by sea round the coast of Asia. The Tatars were riot good navigators, and the Polos at last obtained permission to escort the young princess on the rather perilous voyage. They started in 1292, from Zayton, a port in Fokien, and after a voyage of over two years round the South coast of Asia, successfully carried the lady to her destined home, though she ultimately had to marry the son instead of the father, who had died in the interim. They took leave of her, and travelled through Persia to their own place, which they reached in 1295. When they arrived at the ancestral mansion of the Polos, in their coarse dress of Tatar cut, their relatives for some time refused to believe that they were really the long-lost merchants. But the Polos invited them to a banquet, in which they dressed themselves all in their best, and put on new suits for every course, giving the clothes they had taken off to the servants. At the conclusion of the banquet they brought forth the shabby dresses in which they had first arrived, and taking sharp knives, began to rip up the seams, from which they took vast quantities of rubies, sapphires, carbuncles, diamonds, and emeralds, into which form they had converted most of their property. This exhibition naturally changed the character of the welcome they received from their relatives, who were then eager to learn how they had come by such riches.

In describing the wealth of the Great Khan, Marco Polo, who was the chief spokesman of the party, was obliged to use the numeral "million" to express the amount of his wealth and the number of the population over whom he ruled. This was regarded as part of the usual travellers' tales, and Marco Polo was generally known by his friends as "Messer Marco Millione."

Such a reception of his stories was no great encouragement to Marco to tell the tale of his remarkable travels, but in the year of his arrival at Venice a war broke out between Genoa and the Queen of the Adriatic, in which Marco Polo was captured and cast into prison at Genoa. There he found as a fellow-prisoner one Rusticano of Pisa, a man of some learning and a sort of predecessor of Sir Thomas Malory, since he had devoted much time to re-writing, in prose, abstracts of the many romances relating to the Round Table. These he wrote, not in Italian (which can scarcely be said to have existed for literary purposes in those days), but in French, the common language of chivalry throughout Western Europe. While in prison with Marco Polo, he took down in French the narrative of the great traveller, and thus preserved it for all time. Marco Polo was released in 1299, and returned to Venice, where he died some time after 9th January 1334, the date of his will.

Of the travels thus detailed in Marco Polo's book, and of their importance and significance in the history of geographical discovery, it is impossible to give any adequate account in this place. It will, perhaps, suffice if we give the summary of his claims made out by Colonel Sir Henry Yule, whose edition of his travels is one of the great monuments of English learning:—

"He was the first traveller to trace a route across the whole longitude of Asia, naming and describing kingdom after kingdom which he had seen with his own eyes: the deserts of Persia, the flowering plateaux and wild gorges of Badakhshan, the jade-bearing rivers of Khotan, the Mongolian Steppes, cradle of the power that had so lately threatened to swallow up Christendom, the new and brilliant court that had been established by Cambaluc; the first traveller to reveal China in all its wealth and vastness, its mighty rivers, its huge cities, its rich manufactures, its swarming population, the inconceivably vast fleets that quickened its seas and its inland waters; to tell us of the nations on its borders, with all their eccentricities of manners and worship; of Tibet, with its sordid devotees; of Burma, with its golden pagodas and their tinkling crowns; of Laos, of Siam, of Cochin China, of Japan, the Eastern Thule, with its rosy pearls and golden-roofed palaces; the first to speak of that museum of beauty and wonder, still so imperfectly ransacked, the Indian Archipelago, source of those aromatics then so highly prized, and whose origin was so dark; of Java, the pearl of islands; of Sumatra, with its many kings, its strange costly products, and its cannibal races; of the naked savages of Nicobar and Andaman; of Ceylon, the island of gems, with its sacred mountain, and its tomb of Adam; of India the

Great, not as a dreamland of Alexandrian fables, but as a country seen and personally explored, with its virtuous Brahmans, its obscene ascetics, its diamonds, and the strange tales of their acquisition, its sea-beds of pearl, and its powerful sun: the first in mediæval times to give any distinct account of the secluded Christian empire of Abyssinia, and the semi-Christian island of Socotra; to speak, though indeed dimly, of Zanzibar, with its negroes and its ivory, and of the vast and distant Madagascar, bordering on the dark ocean of the South, with its Ruc and other monstrosities, and, in a remotely opposite region, of Siberia and the Arctic Ocean, of dog-sledges, white bears, and reindeer-riding Tunguses."

Marco Polo's is thus one of the greatest names in the history of geography; it may, indeed, be doubted whether any other traveller has ever added so extensively to our detailed knowledge of the earth's surface. Certainly up to the time of Mr. Stanley no man had on land visited so many places previously unknown to civilised Europe. But the lands he discovered, though already fully populated, were soon to fall into disorder,

and to be closed to any civilising
FRA MAURO'S MAP, 1457. influences. Nothing for a long time followed from these discoveries, and indeed almost up to the present day his accounts were received with incredulity, and he himself was regarded more as "Marco Millione" than as Marco Polo.

Extensive as were Marco Polo's travels, they were yet exceeded in extent, though not in variety, by those of the greatest of Arabian travellers, Mohammed Ibn Batuta, a native of Tangier, who began his travels in 1334, as part of the ordinary duty of a good Mohammedan to visit the holy city of Mecca. While at Alexandria he met a learned sage named Borhan Eddin, to whom he expressed his desire to travel. Borhan said to him, "You must then visit my brother Farid Iddin and my brother Rokn Eddin in Scindia, and my brother Borhan Eddin in China. When you see them, present my compliments to them." Owing mainly to the fact that the Tatar princes had adopted Islamism instead of Christianity, after the failure of Gregory X. to send Christian teachers to China, Ibn Batuta was ultimately enabled to greet all three brothers of Borhan Eddin. Indeed, he performed a more extraordinary exploit, for he was enabled to convey the greetings of the Sheikh Kawan Eddin, whom he met in China, to a relative of his residing in the Soudan. During the thirty years of his travels he visited the Holy Land, Armenia, the Crimea, Constantinople (which he visited in company with a Greek princess, who married one of the Tatar Khans), Bokhara, Afghanistan, and Delhi. Here he found favour with the emperor Mohammed Inghlak, who appointed him a judge, and sent him on an embassy to China, at first overland, but, as this was found too dangerous a route, he went ultimately from Calicut, via Ceylon, the Maldives, and Sumatra, to Zaitun, then the great port of China. Civil war having broken out, he returned by the same route to Calicut, but dared not face the emperor, and went on to Ormuz and Mecca, and returned to Tangier in 1349. But even then his taste for travel had not been exhausted. He soon set out for Spain, and worked his way through Morocco, across the Sahara, to the Soudan. He travelled along the Niger (which he took for the Nile), and visited Timbuctoo. He ultimately returned to Fez in 1353, twenty-eight years after he had set out on his travels. Their chief interest is in showing the wide extent of Islam in his day, and the facilities which a common creed gave for extensive travel. But the account of his journeys was written in Arabic, and had no influence on European knowledge, which, indeed, had little to learn from him after Marco Polo, except with regard to the Soudan. With him the history of mediæval geography may be fairly said to end, for within eighty years of his death began the activity of Prince Henry the Navigator, with whom the modern epoch begins.

Meanwhile India had become somewhat better known, chiefly by the travels of wandering friars, who visited it mainly for the sake of the shrine of St. Thomas, who was supposed to have been martyred in India. Mention should also be made of the early spread of the Nestorian Church throughout Central Asia. As early as the seventh century the Syrian Christians who followed the views of Nestorius began spreading them eastward, founding sees in Persia and Turkestan, and ultimately spreading as far as Pekin. There was a certain revival of their missionary activity under the Mongol Khans, but the restricted nature of the language in which their reports were written prevented them from having any effect upon geographical knowledge, except in one particular, which is of some interest. The fate of the Lost Ten Tribes of Israel has always excited interest, and a legend arose that they had been converted to Christianity, and existed somewhere in the East under a king who was also a priest, and known as Prester John. Now, in the reports brought by some of the Nestorian priests westward, it was stated that one of the Mongol princes named Ung Khan had adopted Christianity, and as this in Syriac sounded something like "John the Cohen," or "Priest," he was identified with the Prester John of legend, and for a long time one of the objects of travel in the East was to discover this Christian kingdom. It was, however, later ascertained that there did exist such a Christian kingdom in Abyssinia, and as owing to the erroneous views of Ptolemy, followed by the Arabs, Abyssinia was considered to spread towards Farther India, the land of Prester John was identified in Abyssinia. We shall see later on how this error helped the progress of geographical discovery.

The total addition of these mediæval travels to geographical knowledge consisted mainly in the addition of a wider extent of land in China, and the archipelago of Japan, or Cipangu, to the map of the world. The accompanying map displays the various travels and voyages of importance, and will enable the reader to understand how students of geography, who added on to Ptolemy's estimate of the extent of the world east and west the new knowledge acquired by Marco Polo, would still further decrease the distance westward between Europe and Cipangu, and thus prepare men for the voyage of Columbus.

[*Authorities:* Sir Henry Yule, *Cathay and the Way Thither*, 1865; *The Book of Ser Marco Polo*, 1875.]

CHAPTER V

ROADS AND COMMERCE

We have now conducted the course of our inquiries through ancient times and the Middle Ages up to the very eve of the great discoveries of the fifteenth and sixteenth centuries, and we have roughly indicated what men had learned about the earth during that long period, and, how they learned it. But it still remains to consider by what means they arrived at their knowledge, and why they sought for it. To some extent we may have answered the latter question when dealing with the progress of conquest, but men did not conquer merely for the sake of conquest. We have still to consider the material advantages attaching to warfare. Again when men go on their wars of discovery, they have to progress, for the most part, along paths already beaten for them by the natives of the country they intend to conquer; and often when they have succeeded in warfare, they have to consolidate their rule by creating new and more appropriate means of communication. To put it shortly, we have still to discuss the roads of the ancient and mediæval worlds, and the commerce for which those roads were mainly used.

A road may be, for our purposes, most readily defined as the most convenient means of communication between two towns; and this logically implies that the towns existed before the roads were made; and in a fuller investigation of any particular roads, it will be necessary to start by investigating why men collect their dwellings at certain definite spots. In the beginning, assemblies of men were made chiefly or altogether for defensive purposes, and the earliest towns were those which, from their natural position, like Athens or Jerusalem, could be most easily defended. Then, again, religious motives often had their influence in early times, and towns would grow round temples or cloisters. But soon considerations of easy accessibility rule in the choice of settlements, and for that purpose towns on rivers, especially at fords of rivers, as Westminster, or in well-protected harbours like Naples, or in the centre of a district, as Nuremberg or Vienna, would form the most convenient places of meeting for exchange of goods. Both on a river, or on the sea-shore, the best means of communication would be by ships or boats; but once such towns had been established, it would be necessary to connect them with one another by land routes, and these would be determined chiefly by the lie of the land. Where mountains interfered, a large detour would have to be made—as, for example, round the Pyrenees; if rivers intervened, fords would have to be sought for, and a new town probably built at the most convenient place of passage. When once a recognised way had been found between any two places, the conservative instincts of man would keep it in existence, even though a better route were afterwards found.

The influence of water communication is of paramount importance in determining the situation of towns in early times. Towns in the corners of bays, like Archangel, Riga, Venice, Genoa, Naples, Tunis, Bassorah, Calcutta, would naturally be the centre-points of the trade of the bay. On rivers a suitable spot would be where the tides ended, like London, or at conspicuous bends of a stream, or at junctures with affluents, as Coblentz or Khartoum. One nearly always finds important towns at the two ends of a peninsula, like Hamburg and Lubeck, Venice and Genoa; though for naval purposes it is desirable to have a station at the head of the peninsula, to command both arms of the sea, as at Cherbourg, Sevastopol, or Gibraltar. Roads would then easily be formed across the base of the peninsula, and to its extreme point.

At first the inhabitants of any single town would regard those of all others as their enemies, but after a time they would find it convenient to exchange some of their superfluities for those of their neighbours, and in this way trade would begin. Markets would become neutral ground, in which mutual animosities would be, for a time, laid aside for the common advantage; and it would often happen that localities on the border line of two states would be chosen as places for the exchange of goods, ultimately giving rise to the existence of a fresh town. As commercial intercourse increased, the very inaccessibility of fortress towns on the heights would cause them to be neglected for settlements in the valleys or by the river sides, and, as a rule, roads pick out valleys or level ground for their natural course. For military purposes, however, it would sometimes be necessary to depart from the valley routes, and, as we shall see, the Roman roads paid no regard to these requirements.

The earliest communication between nations, as we have seen, was that of the Phœnicians by sea. They founded factories, or neutral grounds for trade, at appropriate spots all along the Mediterranean coasts, and the Greeks soon followed their example in the Ægean and Black Seas. But at an early date, as we know from the Bible, caravan routes were established between Egypt, Syria, and Mesopotamia, and later on these were extended into Farther Asia. But in Europe the great road-builders were the Romans. Rome owed its importance in the ancient world to its central position, at first in Italy, and then in the whole of the Mediterranean. It combined almost all the advantages necessary for a town: it was in the bend of a river, yet accessible from the sea; its natural hills made it easily defensible, as Hannibal found to his cost; while its central position in the Latian Plain made it the natural resort of all the Latin traders. The Romans soon found it necessary to utilise their central position by rendering themselves accessible to the rest of Italy, and they commenced building those marvellous roads, which in most cases have remained, owing to their solid construction. "Building" is the proper word to use, for a Roman road is really a broad wall built in a deep ditch so as to come up above the level of the surface. Scarcely any amount of traffic could wear this solid substructure away, and to this day throughout Europe traces can be found of the Roman roads built nearly two thousand years ago. As the Roman Empire extended, these roads formed one of the chief means by which the lords of the world were enabled to preserve their conquests. By placing a legion in a central spot, where many of these roads converged, they were enabled to strike quickly in any direction and overawe the country. Stations were naturally built along these roads, and to the present day many of the chief highways of Europe follow the course of the old Roman roads. Our modern civilisation is in a large measure the outcome of this network of roads, and we can distinctly trace a difference in the culture of a nation where such roads never existed—as in Russia and Hungary, as contrasted with the west of Europe, where they formed the best means of communication. It was only in the neighbourhood of these highways that the fullest information was obtained of the position of towns, and the divisions of peoples; and a sketch map like the one already given, of the chief Roman roads of antiquity, gives also, as it were, a skeleton of the geographical knowledge summed up in the great work of Ptolemy.

But of more importance for the future development of geographical knowledge were the great caravan routes of Asia, to which we must now turn our attention. Asia is the continent of plateaux which culminate in the Steppes of the Pamirs, appropriately called by their inhabitants "the Roof of the World." To the east of these, four great mountain ranges run, roughly, along the parallels of latitude—the Himalayas to the south, the Kuen-Iun, Thian Shan, and Altai to the north. Between the Himalayas and the Kuen-lun is the great Plateau of Tibet, which runs into a sort of cul-de-sac at its western end in Kashmir. Between the Kuen-lun and the Thian Shan we have the Gobi Steppe of Mongolia, running west of Kashgar and Yarkand; while between the Thian Shan and the Altai we have the great Kirghiz Steppe. It is clear that only two routes are possible between Eastern and Western Asia: that between the Kuen-lun and the Thian Shan via Kashgar and Bokhara, and that south of the Altai, skirting the north of the great lakes Balkash, Aral, and Caspian, to the south of Russia. The former would lead to Bassorah or Ormuz, and thence by sea, or overland, round Arabia to Alexandria; the latter and longer route would reach Europe via Constantinople. Communication between Southern Asia and Europe would mainly be by sea, along the coast of the Indies, taking advantage of the monsoons from Ceylon to Aden, and then by the Red

Sea. Alexandria, Bassorah, and Ormuz would thus naturally be the chief centres of Eastern trade, while communication with the Mongols or with China would go along the two routes above mentioned, which appear to have existed during all historic time. It was by these latter routes that the Polos and the other mediæval travellers to Cathay reached that far-distant country. But, as we know from Marco Polo's travels, China could also be reached by the sea voyage; and for all practical purposes, in the late Middle Ages, when the Mongol empire broke up, and traffic through mid Asia was not secure, communication with the East was via Alexandria.

Now it is important for our present inquiry to realise how largely Europe after the Crusades was dependent on the East for most of the luxuries of life. Nothing produced by the looms of Europe could equal the silk of China, the calico of India, the muslin of Mussul. The chief gems which decorated the crowns of kings and nobles, the emerald, the topaz, the ruby, the diamond, all came from the East—mainly from India. The whole of mediæval medical science was derived from the Arabs, who sought most of their drugs from Arabia or India. Even for the incense which burned upon the innumerable altars of Roman Catholic Europe, merchants had to seek the materials in the Levant. For many of the more refined handicrafts, artists had to seek their best material from Eastern traders: such as shellac for varnish, or mastic for artists' colours (gamboge from Cambodia, ultramarine from lapis lazuli); while it was often necessary, under mediæval circumstances, to have resort to the musk or opopanax of the East to counteract the odours resulting from the bad sanitary habits of the West. But above all, for the condiments which were almost necessary for health, and certainly desirable for seasoning the salted food of winter and the salted fish of Lent. Europeans were dependent upon the spices of the Asiatic islands. In Hakluyt's great work on "English Voyages and Navigations," he gives in his second volume a list, written out by an Aleppo merchant, William Barrett, in 1584, of the places whence the chief staples of the Eastern trade came, and it will be interesting to give a selection from his long account.

> Cloves from Maluco, Tarenate, Amboyna, by way of Java.
> Nutmegs from Banda.
> Maces from Banda, Java, and Malacca.
> Pepper Common from Malabar.
> Sinnamon from Seilan (Ceylon).
> Spicknard from Zindi (Scinde) and Lahor.
> Ginger Sorattin from Sorat (Surat) within Cambaia (Bay of Bengal).
> Corall of Levant from Malabar.
> Sal Ammoniacke from Zindi and Cambaia.

Camphora from Brimeo (Borneo) near to China.
Myrrha from Arabia Felix.
Borazo (Borax) from Cambaia and Lahor.
Ruvia to die withall, from Chalangi.
Allumme di Rocca (Rock Alum) from China and
Constantinople.
Oppopanax from Persia.
Lignum Aloes from Cochin, China, and Malacca.
Laccha (Shell-lac) from Pegu and Balaguate.
Agaricum from Alemannia. Bdellium from Arabia Felix.
Tamarinda from Balsara (Bassorah).
Safran (Saffron) from Balsara and Persia.
Thus from Secutra (Socotra).
Nux Vomica from Malabar.
Sanguis Draconis (Dragon's Blood) from Secutra.
Musk from Tartarie by way of China.
Indico (Indigo) from Zindi and Cambaia.
Silkes Fine from China.
Castorium (Castor Oil) from Almania.
Masticke from Sio.
Oppium from Pugia (Pegu) and Cambaia.
Dates from Arabia Felix and Alexandria.
Sena from Mecca.
Gumme Arabicke from Zaffo (Jaffa).
Ladanum (Laudanum) from Cyprus and Candia.
Lapis Lazzudis from Persia.
Auripigmentum (Gold Paint) from many places of Turkey.
Rubarbe from Persia and China.

These are only a few selections from Barrett's list, but will sufficiently indicate what a large number of household luxuries, and even necessities, were derived from Asia in the Middle Ages. The Arabs had practically the monopoly of this trade, and as Europe had scarcely anything to offer in exchange except its gold and silver coins, there was a continuous drain of the precious metals from West to East, rendering the Sultans and Caliphs continuously richer, and culminating in the splendours of Solomon the Magnificent. Alexandria was practically the centre of all this trade, and most of the nations of Europe found it necessary to establish factories in that city, to safeguard the interests of their merchants, who all sought for Eastern luxuries in its port Benjamin of Tudela, a Jew, who visited it about 1172, gives the following description of it:—

"The city is very mercantile, and affords an excellent market to all nations. People from all Christian kingdoms resort to Alexandria, from

Valencia, Tuscany, Lombardy, Apulia, Amalfi, Sicilia, Raguvia, Catalonia, Spain, Roussillon, Germany, Saxony, Denmark, England, Flandres, Hainault, Normandy, France, Poitou, Anjou, Burgundy, Mediana, Provence, Genoa, Pisa, Gascony, Arragon, and Navarre. From the West you meet Mohammedans from Andalusia, Algarve, Africa, and Arabia, as well as from the countries towards India, Savila, Abyssinia, Nubia, Yemen, Mesopotamia, and Syria, besides Greeks and Turks. From India they import all sorts of spices, which are bought by Christian merchants. The city is full of bustle, and every nation has its own fonteccho (or hostelry) there."

Of all these nations, the Italians had the shortest voyage to make before reaching Alexandria, and the Eastern trade practically fell into their hands before the end of the thirteenth century. At first Amalfi and Pisa were the chief ports, and, as we have seen, it was at Amalfi that the mariner's compass was perfected; but soon the two maritime towns at the heads of the two seas surrounding Italy came to the front, owing to the advantages of their natural position. Genoa and Venice for a long time competed with one another for the monopoly of this trade, but the voyage from Venice was more direct, and after a time Genoa had to content itself with the trade with Constantinople and the northern overland route from China. From Venice the spices, the jewels, the perfumes, and stuffs of the East were transmitted north through Augsburg and Nürnberg to Antwerp and Bruges and the Hanse Towns, receiving from them the gold they had gained by their fisheries and textile goods. England sent her wool to Italy, in order to tickle her palate and her nose with the condiments and perfumes of the East.

The wealth and importance of Venice were due almost entirely to this monopoly of the lucrative Eastern trade. By the fifteenth century she had extended her dominions all along the lower valley of the Po, into Dalmatia, parts of the Morea, and in Crete, till at last, in 1489, she obtained possession of Cyprus, and thus had stations all the way from Aleppo or Alexandria to the north of the Adriatic. But just as she seemed to have reached the height of her prosperity—when the Aldi were the chief printers in Europe, and the Bellini were starting the great Venetian school of painting—a formidable rival came to the front, who had been slowly preparing a novel method of competition in the Eastern trade for nearly the whole of the fifteenth century. With that method begins the great epoch of modern geographical discovery.

[*Authorities:* Heyd, *Commerce du Levant*, 2 vols., 1878.]

CHAPTER VI

TO THE INDIES EASTWARD—PRINCE HENRY AND VASCO DA GAMA

Up to the fifteenth century the inhabitants of the Iberian Peninsula were chiefly occupied in slowly moving back the tide of Mohammedan conquest, which had spread nearly throughout the country from 711 onwards. The last sigh of the Moor in Spain was to be uttered in 1492—an epoch-making year, both in history and in geography. But Portugal, the western side of the peninsula, had got rid of her Moors at a much earlier date—more that 200 years before—though she found it difficult to preserve her independence from the neighbouring kingdom of Castile. The attempt of King Juan of Castile to conquer the country was repelled by João, a natural son of the preceding king of Portugal, and in 1385 he became king, and freed Portugal from any danger on the side of Castile by his victory at Aljubarrota. He married Philippa, daughter of John of Gaunt; and his third son, Henry, was destined to be the means of revolutionising men's views of the inhabited globe. He first showed his mettle in the capture of Ceuta, opposite Gibraltar, at the time of the battle of Agincourt, 1415, and by this means he first planted the Portuguese banner on the Moorish coast. This contact with the Moors may possibly have first suggested to Prince Henry the idea of planting similar factory-fortresses among the Mussulmans of India; but, whatever the cause, he began, from about the year 1418, to devote all his thoughts and attention to the possibility of reaching India otherwise than through the known routes, and for that purpose established himself on the rocky promontory of Sagres, almost the most western spot on the continent of Europe.

Here he established an observatory, and a seminary for the training of theoretical and practical navigators. He summoned thither astronomers and cartographers and skilled seamen, while he caused stouter and larger vessels to be built for the express purpose of exploration. He perfected the astrolabe (the clumsy predecessor of the modern sextant) by which the latitude could be with some accuracy determined; and he equipped all his ships with the compass, by which their steering was entirely determined. He brought from Majorca (which, as we have seen, was the centre of practical map-making in the fourteenth century) one Mestre Jacme, "a man very skilful in the art of navigation, and in the making of maps and instruments." With his aid, and doubtless that of others, he set himself to study the problem of the possibility of a sea voyage to India round the coast of Africa.

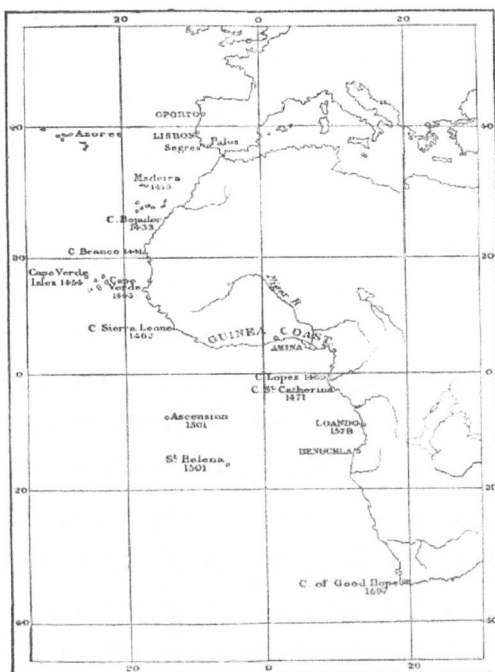

PROGRESS OF PORTUGUESE DISCOVERY

We have seen that Ptolemy, with true scientific caution, had left undefined the extent of Africa to the south; but Eratosthenes and many of the Roman geographers, even after Ptolemy, were not content with this agnosticism, but boldly assumed that the coast of Africa made a semicircular sweep from the right horn of Africa, just south of the Red Sea, with which they were acquainted, round to the north-western shore, near what we now term Morocco. If this were the fact, the voyage by the ocean along this sweep of shore would be even shorter than the voyage through the Mediterranean and Red Seas, while of course there would be no need for disembarking at the Isthmus of Suez. The writers who thus curtailed Africa of its true proportions assumed another continent south of it, which, however, was in the torrid zone, and completely uninhabitable.

Now the north-west coast of Africa was known in Prince Henry's days as far as Cape Bojador. It would appear that Norman sailors had already advanced beyond Cape Non, or Nun, which was so called because it was supposed that nothing existed beyond it. Consequently the problems that Prince Henry had to solve were whether the coast of Africa trended sharply to the east after Cape Bojador, and whether the ideas of the ancients about the uninhabitability of the torrid zone were justified by fact. He attempted to solve these problems by sending out, year after year, expeditions down the north-west coast of Africa, each of which penetrated farther than its predecessor. Almost at the beginning he was rewarded by the discovery, or re-discovery, of Madeira in 1420, by João Gonsalvez Zarco, one of the squires of his household. For some time he was content with occupying this and the neighbouring island of Porto Santo, which, however, was ruined by the rabbits let loose upon it. On Madeira vines from Burgundy were planted, and to this day form the chief industry of the island. In 1435 Cape Bojador was passed, and in 1441 Cape Branco discovered. Two years later Cape Verde was reached and passed by Nuno Tristão, and for the first time there were signs that the African coast trended eastward. By this time Prince Henry's men had become familiar with the natives along the shore and no less than one thousand of them had been brought back and distributed among the Portuguese nobles as pages and attendants. In 1455 a Venetian, named Alvez Cadamosto, undertook a voyage still farther south for purposes of trade, the Prince supplying the capital, and covenanting for half profits on results. They reached the mouth of the Gambia, but found the natives hostile. Here for the first time European navigators lost sight of the pole-star and saw the brilliant constellation of the Southern Cross. The last discovery made during Prince Henry's life was that of the Cape Verde Islands, by one of his captains, Diogo Gomez, in 1460—the very year of his death. As the successive discoveries were made, they were jotted down by the Prince's cartographers on portulanos, and just before his death the King of Portugal sent to a Venetian monk, Fra Mauro, details of all discoveries up to that time, to be recorded on a *mappa mundi*, a copy of which still exists (p. 77).

The impulse thus given by Prince Henry's patient investigation of the African coast continued long after his death. In 1471 Fernando de Poo discovered the island which now bears his name, while in the same year Pedro d'Escobar crossed the equator. Wherever the Portuguese investigators landed they left marks of their presence, at first by erecting crosses, then by carving on trees Prince Henry's motto, "Talent de bien faire," and finally they adopted the method of erecting stone pillars, surmounted by a cross, and inscribed with the king's arms and name. These pillars were called *padraos*. In 1484, Diego Cam, a knight of the king's household, set up one of these pillars at the mouth of a large river, which he therefore called the Rio do Padrao; it was called by the natives the Zaire, and is now known as the River Congo. Diego Cam was, on this expedition, accompanied by Martin Behaim of Nürnberg, whose globe is celebrated in geographical history as the last record of the older views (p. 115).

Meanwhile, from one of the envoys of the native kings who visited the Portuguese Court, information was received that far to the east of the countries hitherto discovered there was a great Christian king. This brought to mind the mediæval tradition of Prester John, and accordingly the

Portuguese determined to make a double attempt, both by sea and by land, to reach this monarch. By sea the king sent two vessels under the command of Bartholomew Diaz, while by land he despatched, in the following year, two men acquainted with Arabic, Pedro di Covilham and Affonso de Payba. Covilham reached Aden, and there took ship for Calicut, being the first Portuguese to sail the Indian Ocean. He then returned to Sofala, and obtained news of the Island of the Moon, now known as Madagascar. With this information he returned to Cairo, where he found ambassadors from João, two Jews, Abraham of Beja and Joseph of Lamejo. These he sent back with the information that ships that sailed down the coast of Guinea would surely reach the end of Africa, and when they arrived in the Eastern Ocean they should ask for Sofala and the Island of the Moon. Meanwhile Covilham returned to the Red Sea, and made his way into Abyssinia, where he married and settled down, transmitting from time to time information to Portugal which gave Europeans their first notions of Abyssinia.

The voyage by land in search of Prester John had thus been completely successful, while, at the same time, information had been obtained giving certain hopes of the voyage by sea. This had, in its way, been almost as successful, for Diaz had rounded the cape now known as the Cape of Good Hope, but to which he proposed giving the title of Cabo Tormentoso, or "Stormy Cape." King João, however, recognising that Diaz's voyage had put the seal upon the expectations with which Prince Henry had, seventy years before, started his series of explorations, gave it the more auspicious name by which it is now known.

For some reason which has not been adequately explained, no further attempt was made for nearly ten years to carry out the final consummation of Prince Henry's plan by sending out another expedition. In the meantime, as we shall see, Columbus had left Portugal, after a mean attempt had been made by the king to carry out his novel plan of reaching India without his aid; and, as a just result, the discovery of a western voyage to the Indies (as it was then thought) had been successfully accomplished by Columbus, in the service of the Catholic monarchs of Spain, in 1492. This would naturally give pause to any attempt at reaching India by the more cumbersome route of coasting along Africa, which had turned out to be a longer process than Prince Henry had thought. Three years after Columbus's discovery King João died, and his son and successor Emmanuel did not take up the traditional Portuguese method of reaching India till the third year of his reign.

By this time it had become clear, from Columbus's second voyage, that there were more difficulties in the way of reaching the Indies by his method than had been thought; and the year after his return from his second voyage in 1496, King Emmanuel determined on once more taking up the older method. He commissioned Vasco da Gama, a gentleman of his court, to attempt the eastward route to India with three vessels, carrying in all about sixty men. Already by this time Columbus's bold venture into the unknown seas had encouraged similar boldness in others, and instead of coasting down the whole extent of the western coast of Africa, Da Gama steered direct for Cape Verde Islands, and thence out into the ocean, till he reached the Bay of St. Helena, a little to the north of the Cape of Good Hope.

For a time he was baffled in his attempt to round the Cape by the strong south-easterly winds, which blow there continually during the summer season; but at last he commenced coasting along the eastern shores of Africa, and at every suitable spot he landed some of his sailors to make inquiries about Covilham and the court of Prester John. But in every case he found the ports inhabited by fanatical Moors, who, as soon as they discovered that their visitors were Christians, attempted to destroy them, and refused to supply them with pilots for the further voyage to India. This happened at Mozambique, at Quiloa, and at Mombasa, and it was not till he arrived at Melinda that he was enabled to obtain provisions and a pilot, Malemo Cana, an Indian of Guzerat, who was quite familiar with the voyage to Calicut. Under his guidance Gama's fleet went from Melinda to Calicut in twenty-three days. Here the Zamorin, or sea-king, displayed the same antipathy to his Christian visitors. The Mohammedan traders of the place recognised at once the dangerous rivalry which the visit of the Portuguese implied, with their monopoly of the Eastern trade, and represented Gama and his followers as merely pirates. Vasco, however, by his firm behaviour, managed to evade the machinations of his trade rivals, and induced the Zamorin to regard favourably an alliance with the Portuguese king. Contenting himself with this result, he embarked again, and after visiting Melinda, the only friendly spot he had found on the east coast of Africa, he returned to Lisbon in September 1499, having spent no less than two years on the voyage. King Emmanuel received him with great favour, and appointed him Admiral of the Indies.

The significance of Vasco da Gama's voyage was at once seen by the persons whose trade monopoly it threatened—the Venetians, and the Sultan of Egypt. Priuli, the Venetian chronicler, reports: "When this news reached Venice the whole city felt it greatly, and remained stupefied, and the wisest held it as the worst news that had ever arrived"—as indeed they might, for it prophesied the downfall of the Venetian Empire. The Sultan of Egypt was equally moved, for the greatest source of his riches was derived from the duty of five per cent. which he levied on all merchandise entering his dominions, and ten per cent. upon all goods exported from them. Hitherto there had been all manner of bickerings between Venice and Egypt, but this common danger brought them together. The Sultan represented to Venice the need of common action in order to drive away the new commerce; but Egypt was without a navy, and had indeed no wood suitable for shipbuilding. The Venetians took the trouble to transmit wood to Cairo, which was then carried by camels to Suez, where a small fleet was prepared to attack the Portuguese on their next visit to the Indian Ocean.

The Portuguese had in the meantime followed up Vasco da Gama's voyage with another attempt, which was, in its way, even more important. In 1500 the king sent no less than thirteen ships under the command of Pedro Alvarez Cabral, with Franciscans to convert, and twelve hundred fighting men to overawe, the Moslems of the Indian Ocean. He determined on steering even a more westerly course than Vasco da Gama, and when he arrived in 17° south of the line, he discovered land which he took possession of in the name of Portugal, and named Santa Cruz. The actual cross which he erected on this occasion is still preserved in Brazil, for Cabral had touched upon the land now known by that name. It is true that one of Columbus's companions, Pinzon, had already touched upon the coast of Brazil before Cabral, but it is evident from his experience that, even apart from Columbus, the Portuguese would have discovered the New World sooner or later. It is, however, to be observed that in stating this, as all historians do, they leave out of account the fact that, but for Columbus, sailors would still have continued the old course of coasting along the shore, by which they would never have left the Old World. Cabral lost several of his ships and many of his men, and, though he brought home a rich cargo, was not regarded as successful, and Vasco da Gama was again sent out with a large fleet in 1502, with which he conquered the Zamorin of Calicut and obtained rich treasures. In subsidiary voyages the Portuguese navigators discovered the islands of St. Helena, Ascension, the Seychelles, Socotra, Tristan da Cunha, the Maldives, and Madagascar.

Meanwhile King Emmanuel was adopting the Venetian method of colonisation, which consisted in sending a Vice-Doge to each of its colonies for a term of two years, during which his duty was to encourage trade and to collect tribute. In a similar way, Emmanuel appointed a Viceroy for his Eastern trade, and in 1505 Almeida had settled in Ceylon, with a view to monopolising the cinnamon trade of that place.

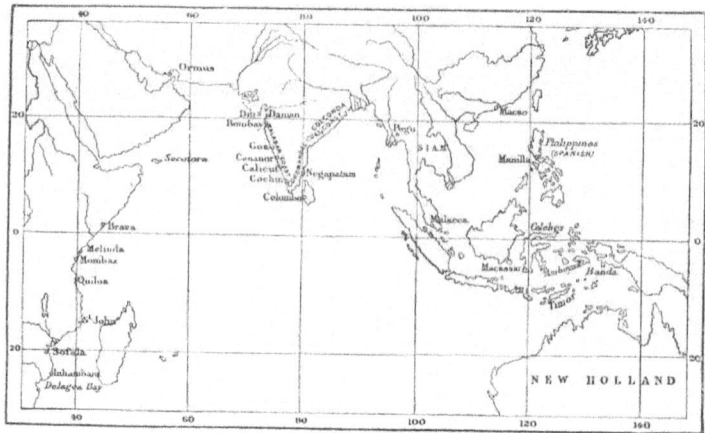

PORTUGUESE INDIES

But the greatest of the Portuguese viceroys was Affonso de Albuquerque, who captured the important post of Goa, on the mainland of India, which still belongs to Portugal, and the port of Ormuz, which, we have seen, was one of the centres of the Eastern trade. Even more important was the capture of the Moluccas, or Spice Islands, which were discovered in 1511, after the Portuguese had seized Malacca. By 1521 the Portuguese had full possession of the Spice Islands, and thus held the trade of condiments entirely in their own hands. The result was seen soon in the rise of prices in the European markets. Whereas at the end of the fifteenth century pepper, for instance, was about 17s. a pound, from 1521 and onwards its average price grew to be 25s., and so with almost all the ingredients by which food could be made more tasty. One of the circumstances, however, which threw the monopoly into the hands of the Portuguese was the seizure of Egypt in 1521 by the Turks under Selim I., which would naturally derange the course of trade from its old route through Alexandria. From the Moluccas easy access was found to China, and ultimately to Japan, so that the Portuguese for a time held in their hands the whole of the Eastern trade, on which Europe depended for most of its luxuries.

As we shall see, the Portuguese only won by a neck—if we may use a sporting expression—in the race for the possession of the Spice Islands. In the very year they obtained possession of them, Magellan, on his way round the world, had reached the Philippines, within a few hundred miles of them, and his ship, the *Victoria*, actually sailed through them that year. In fact, 1521 is a critical year in the discovery of the world, for both the Spanish and Portuguese (the two nations who had attempted to reach the Indies eastward and westward) arrived at the goal of their desires, the Spice Islands, in that same year, while the closure of Egypt to commerce occurred opportunely to divert the trade into the hands of the Portuguese.

Finally, the year 1521 was signalised by the death of King Emmanuel of Portugal, under whose auspices the work of Prince Henry the Navigator was completed.

It must here be observed that we are again anticipating matters. As soon as the discovery of the New World was announced, the Pope was appealed to, to determine the relative shares of Spain and Portugal in the discoveries which would clearly follow upon Columbus's voyage. By his Bull, dated 4th May 1493, Alexander VI. granted all discoveries to the west to Spain, leaving it to be understood that all to the east belonged to Portugal. The line of demarcation was an imaginary one drawn from pole to pole, and passing one hundred leagues west of the Azores and Cape Verde Islands, which were supposed, in the inaccurate geography of the time, to be in the same meridian. In the following year the Portuguese monarch applied for a revision of the *raya*, as this would keep him out of all discovered in the New World altogether; and the line of demarcation was then shifted 270 leagues westward, or altogether 1110 miles west of the Cape Verdes. By a curious coincidence, within six years Cabral had discovered Brazil, which fell within the angle thus cut off by the *raya* from South America. Or was it entirely a coincidence? May not Cabral have been directed to take this unusually westward course in order to ascertain if any land fell within the Portuguese claims? When, however, the Spice Islands were discovered, it remained to be discussed whether the line of demarcation, when continued on the other side of the globe, brought them within the Spanish or Portuguese "sphere of influence," as we should say nowadays. By a curious chance they happened to be very near the line, and, with the inaccurate maps of the period, a pretty subject of quarrel was afforded between the Portuguese and Spanish commissioners who met at Badajos to determine the question. This was left undecided by the Junta, but by a family compact, in 1529, Charles V. ceded to his brother-in-law, the King of Portugal, any rights he might have to the Moluccas, for the sum of 350,000 gold ducats, while he himself retained the Philippines, which have been Spanish ever since.

By this means the Indian Ocean became, for all trade purposes, a Portuguese lake throughout the sixteenth century, as will be seen from the preceding map, showing the trading stations of the Portuguese all along the shores of the ocean. But they only possessed their monopoly for fifty years, for in 1580 the Spanish and Portuguese crowns became united on the head of Philip II., and by the time Portugal recovered its independence, in 1640, serious rivals had arisen to compete with her and Spain for the monopoly of the Eastern trade.

[*Authorities*: Major, *Prince Henry the Navigator*, 1869; Beazeley, *Prince Henry the Navigator*, 1895; F. Hummerich, *Vasco da Gama*, 1896.]

CHAPTER VII

TO THE INDIES WESTWARD—THE SPANISH ROUTE—
COLUMBUS AND MAGELLAN

While the Portuguese had, with slow persistency, devoted nearly a century to carrying out Prince Henry's idea of reaching the Indies by the eastward route, a bold yet simple idea had seized upon a Genoese sailor, which was intended to achieve the same purpose by sailing westward. The ancients, as we have seen, had recognised the rotundity of the earth, and Eratosthenes had even recognised the possibility of reaching India by sailing westward. Certain traditions of the Greeks and the Irish had placed mysterious islands far out to the west in the Atlantic, and the great philosopher Plato had imagined a country named Atlantis, far out in the Indian Ocean, where men were provided with all the gifts of nature. These views of the ancients came once more to the attention of the learned, owing to the invention of printing and the revival of learning, when the Greek masterpieces began to be made accessible in Latin, chiefly by fugitive Greeks from Constantinople, which had been taken by the Turks in 1453. Ptolemy's geography was printed at Rome in 1462, and with maps in 1478. But even without the maps the calculation which he had made of the length of the known world tended to shorten the distance between Portugal and Farther India by 2500 miles. Since his time the travels of Marco Polo had added to the knowledge of Europe the vast extent of Cathay and the distant islands of Zipangu (Japan), which would again reduce the distance by another 1500 miles. As the Greek geographers had somewhat under-estimated the whole circuit of the globe, it would thus seem that Zipangu was not more than 4000 miles to the west of Portugal. As the Azores were considered to be much farther off from the coast than they really were, it might easily seem, to an enthusiastic mind, that Farther India might be reached when 3000 miles of the ocean had been traversed.

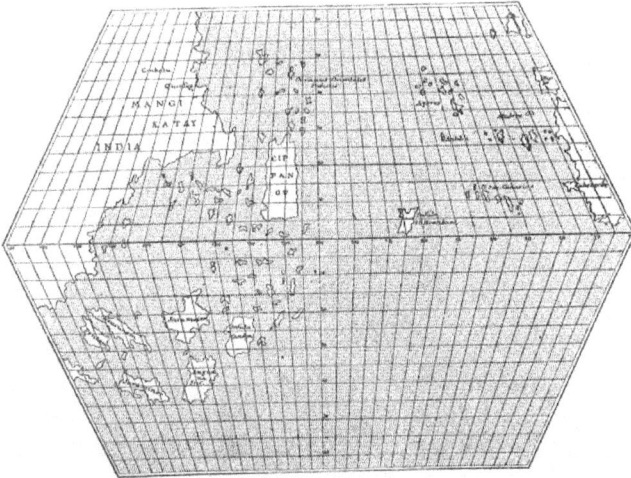

TOSCANELLI'S MAP (*restored*)

This was the notion that seized the mind of Christopher Columbus, born at Genoa in 1446, of humble parentage, his father being a weaver. He seems to have obtained sufficient knowledge to enable him to study the works of the learned, and of the ancients in Latin translations. But in his early years he devoted his attention to obtaining a practical acquaintance with seamanship. In his day, as we have seen, Portugal was the centre of geographical knowledge, and he and his brother Bartolomeo, after many voyages north and south, settled at last in Lisbon—his brother as a map-maker, and himself as a practical seaman. This was about the year 1473, and shortly afterwards he married Felipa Moñiz, daughter of Bartolomeo Perestrello, an Italian in the service of the King of Portugal, and for some time Governor of Madeira.

Now it chanced just at this time that there was a rumour in Portugal that a certain Italian philosopher, named Toscanelli, had put forth views as to the possibility of a westward voyage to Cathay, or China, and the Portuguese king had, through a monk named Martinez, applied to Toscanelli to know his views, which were given in a letter dated 25th June 1474. It would appear that, quite independently, Columbus had heard the rumour, and applied to Toscanelli, for in the latter's reply he, like a good business man, shortened his answer by giving a copy of the letter he had recently written to Martinez. What was more important and more useful, Toscanelli sent a map showing in hours (or degrees) the probable distance between Spain and Cathay westward. By adding the information given by Marco Polo to the incorrect views of Ptolemy about the breadth of the inhabited world, Toscanelli reduced the distance from the Azores to 52°, or 3120 miles. Columbus always expressed his indebtedness to Toscanelli's map for his guidance, and, as we shall see, depended upon it very closely, both in steering, and in estimating the distance to be traversed. Unfortunately this map has been lost, but from a list of geographical positions, with latitude and longitude, founded upon it, modern geographers have been able to restore it in some detail, and a simplified sketch of it may be here inserted, as perhaps the most important document in Columbus's career.

Certainly, whether he had the idea of reaching the Indies by a westward voyage before or not, he adopted Toscanelli's views with enthusiasm, and devoted his whole life henceforth to trying to carry them into operation.

He gathered together all the information he could get about the fabled islands of the Atlantic—the Island of St. Brandan, where that Irish saint found happy mortals; and the Island of Antilla, imagined by others, with its seven cities. He gathered together all the gossip he could hear—of mysterious corpses cast ashore on the Canaries, and resembling no race of men known to Europe; of huge canes, found on the shores of the same islands, evidently carved by man's skill. Curiously enough, these pieces of evidence were logically rather against the existence of a westward route to the Indies than not, since they indicated an unknown race, but, to an enthusiastic mind like Columbus's, anything helped to confirm him in his fixed idea, and besides, he could always reply that these material signs were from the unknown island of Zipangu, which Marco Polo had described as at some distance from the shores of Cathay.

He first approached, as was natural, the King of Portugal, in whose land he was living, and whose traditional policy was directed to maritime exploration. But the Portuguese had for half a century been pursuing another method of reaching India, and were not inclined to take up the novel idea of a stranger, which would traverse their long-continued policy of coasting down Africa. A hearing, however, was given to him, but the report was unfavourable, and Columbus had to turn his eyes elsewhere. There is a tradition that the Portuguese monarch and his advisers thought rather more of Columbus's ideas at first; and attempted secretly to put them into execution; but the pilot to whom they entrusted the proposed voyage lost heart as soon as he lost sight of land, and returned with an adverse verdict on the scheme. It is not known whether Columbus heard of this mean attempt to forestall him, but we find him in 1487 being assisted by the Spanish Court, and from that time for the next five years he was occupied in attempting to induce the Catholic monarchs of Spain, Ferdinand and Isabella, to allow him to try his novel plan of reaching the Indies. The final operations in expelling the Moors from Spain just then engrossed all their attention and all their capital, and Columbus was reduced to despair, and was about to give up all hopes of succeeding in Spain, when one of the great financiers, a converted Jew named Luis de

Santaguel, offered to find means for the voyage, and Columbus was recalled.

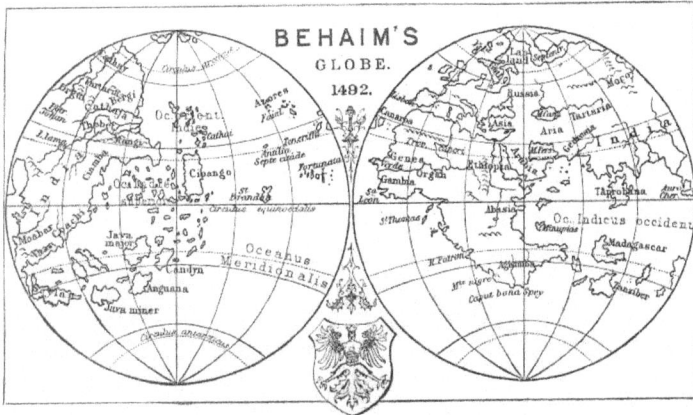

BEHAIM'S GLOBE. 1492.

On the 19th April 1492 articles were signed, by which Columbus received from the Spanish monarchs the titles of Admiral and Viceroy of all the lands he might discover, as well as one-tenth of all the tribute to be derived from them; and on Friday the 3rd August, of the same year, he set sail in three vessels, entitled the *Santa Maria* (the flagship), the *Pinta*, and the *Nina*. He started from the port of Palos, first for the Canary Islands. These he left on the 6th September, and steered due west. On the 13th of that month, Columbus observed that the needle of the compass pointed due north, and thus drew attention to the variability of the compass. By the 21st September his men became mutinous and tried to force him to return. He induced them to continue, and four days afterwards the cry of "Land! land!" was heard, which kept up their spirits for several days, till, on the 1st October, large numbers of birds were seen. By that time Columbus had reckoned that he had gone some 710 leagues from the Canaries, and if Zipangu were in the position that Tostanelli's map gave it, he ought to have been in its neighbourhood. It was reckoned in those days that a ship on an average could make four knots an hour, dead reckoning, which would give about 100 miles a day, so that Columbus might reckon on passing over the 3100 miles which he thought intervened between the Azores and Japan in about thirty-three days. All through the early days of October his courage was kept up by various signs of the nearness of land—birds and branches—while on the 11th October, at sunset, they sounded, and found bottom; and at ten o'clock, Columbus, sitting in the stern of his vessel, saw a light, the first sure sign of land after thirty-five days, and in near enough approximation to Columbus's reckoning to confirm him in the impression that he was approaching the mysterious land of Zipangu. Next morning they landed on an island, called by the natives Guanahain, and by Columbus San Salvador. This has been identified as Watling Island. His first inquiry was as to the origin of the little plates of gold which he saw in the ears of the natives. They replied that they came from the West— another confirmation of his impression. Steering westward, they arrived at Cuba, and afterwards at Hayti (St. Domingo). Here, however, the *Santa Maria* sank, and Columbus determined to return, to bring the good news, after leaving some of his men in a fort at Hayti. The return journey was made in the *Nina* in even shorter time to the Azores, but afterwards severe storms arose, and it was not till the 15th March 1493 that he reached Palos, after an absence of seven and a half months, during which everybody thought that he and his ships had disappeared.

He was naturally received with great enthusiasm by the Spaniards, and after a solemn entry at Barcelona he presented to Ferdinand and Isabella the store of gold and curiosities carried by some of the natives of the islands he had visited. They immediately set about fitting out a much larger fleet of seven vessels, which started from Cadiz, 25th September 1493. He took a more southerly course, but again reached the islands now known as the West Indies. On visiting Hayti he found the fort destroyed, and no traces of the men he had left there. It is needless for our purposes to go through the miserable squabbles which occurred on this and his subsequent voyages, which resulted in Columbus's return to Spain in chains and disgrace. It is only necessary for us to say that in his third voyage, in 1498, he touched on Trinidad, and saw the coast of South America, which he supposed to be the region of the Terrestrial Paradise. This was placed by the mediæval maps at the extreme east of the Old World. Only on his fourth voyage, in 1502, did he actually touch the mainland, coasting along the shores of Central America in the neighbourhood of Panama. After many disappointments, he died, 20th May 1506, at Valladolid, believing, as far as we can judge, to the day of his death, that what he had discovered was what he set out to seek—a westward route to the Indies, though his proud epitaph indicates the contrary:—

A Castilla y á Leon | To Castille and to Leon

Nuevo mondo dió Colon. | A NEW WORLD gave Colon.[1]

[Footnote 1: Columbus's Spanish name was Cristoval Colon.]

To this day his error is enshrined in the name we give to the Windward and Antilles Islands—West Indies: in other words, the Indies reached by the westward route. If they had been the Indies at all, they would have been the most easterly of them.

Even if Columbus had discovered a new route to Farther India, he could not, as we have seen, claim the merit of having originated the idea, which, even in detail, he had taken from Toscanelli. But his claim is even a greater one. He it was who first dared to traverse unknown seas without coasting along the land, and his example was the immediate cause of all the remarkable discoveries that followed his earlier voyages. As we have seen, both Vasco da Gama and Cabral immediately after departed from the slow coasting route, and were by that means enabled to carry out to the full the ideas of Prince Henry; but whereas, by the Portuguese method of coasting, it had taken nearly a century to reach the Cape of Good Hope, within thirty years of Columbus's first venture the whole globe had been circumnavigated.

The first aim of his successors was to ascertain more clearly what it was that Columbus had discovered. Immediately after Columbus's third, voyage, in 1498, and after the news of Vasco da Gama's successful passage to the Indies had made it necessary to discover some strait leading from the "West Indies" to India itself, a Spanish gentleman, named Hojeda, fitted out an expedition at his own expense, with an Italian pilot on board, named Amerigo Vespucci, and tried once more to find a strait to India near Trinidad. They were, of course, unsuccessful, but they coasted along and landed on the north coast of South America, which, from certain resemblances, they termed Little Venice (Venezuela). Next year, as we have seen, Cabral, in following Vasco da Gama, hit upon Brazil, which turned out to be within the Portuguese "sphere of influence," as determined by the line of demarcation.

But, three months previous to Cabral's touching upon Brazil, one of Columbus's companions on his first voyage, Vincenta Yanez Pinzon, had touched on the coast of Brazil, eight degrees south of the line, and from there had worked northward, seeking for a passage which would lead west to the Indies. He discovered the mouth of the Amazon, but, losing two of his vessels, returned to Palos, which he reached in September 1500.

This discovery of an unknown and unsuspected continent so far south of the line created great interest, and shortly after Cabral's return Amerigo Vespucci was sent out in 1501 by the King of Portugal as pilot of a fleet which should explore the new land discovered by Cabral and claim it for the Crown of Portugal. His instructions were to ascertain how much of it was within the line of demarcation. Vespucci reached the Brazilian coast at Cape St. Roque, and then explored it very thoroughly right down to the river La Plata, which was too far west to come within the Portuguese sphere. Amerigo and his companions struck out south-eastward till they reached the island of St. Georgia, 1200 miles east of Cape Horn, where the cold and the floating ice drove them back, and they returned to Lisbon, after having gone farthest south up to their time.

This voyage of Amerigo threw a new light upon the nature of the discovery made by Columbus. Whereas he had thought he had discovered a route to India and had touched upon Farther India, Amerigo and his companions had shown that there was a hitherto unsuspected land intervening between Columbus's discoveries and the long-desired Spice

AMERIGO VESPUCCI.

Islands of Farther India. Amerigo, in describing his discoveries, ventured so far as to suggest that they constituted a New World; and a German professor, named Martin Waldseemüller, who wrote an introduction to Cosmography in 1506, which included an account of Amerigo's discoveries, suggested that this New World should be called after him, AMERICA, after the analogy of Asia, Africa, and Europe. For a long time the continent which we now know as South America was called simply the New World, and was supposed to be joined on to the east coast of Asia. The name America was sometimes applied to it—not altogether inappropriately, since it was Amerigo's voyage which definitely settled that really new lands had been discovered by the western route; and when it was further ascertained that this new land was joined, not to Asia, but to another continent as large as itself, the two new lands were distinguished as North and South America.

It was, at any rate, clear from Amerigo's discovery that the westward route to the Spice Islands would have to be through or round this New World discovered by him, and a Portuguese noble, named Fernao Magelhaens, was destined to discover the practicability of this route. He had served his native country under Almeida and Albuquerque in the East Indies, and was present at the capture of Malacca in 1511, and from that port was despatched by Albuquerque with three ships to visit the far-famed Spice Islands. They visited Amboyna and Banda, and learned enough of the abundance and cheapness of the spices of the islands to recognise their importance; but under the direction of Albuquerque, who only sent them out on an exploring expedition, they returned to him, leaving behind them, however, one of Magelhaens' greatest friends, Francisco Serrao, who settled in Ternate and from time to time sent glowing accounts of the Moluccas to his friend Magelhaens. He in the meantime returned to Portugal, and was employed on an expedition to Morocco. He was not, however, well treated by the Portuguese monarch, and determined to leave his service for that of Charles V., though he made it a condition of his entering his service that he should make no discoveries within the boundaries of the King of Portugal, and do nothing prejudicial to his interests.

This was in the year 1517, and two years elapsed before Magelhaens started on his celebrated voyage. He had represented to the Emperor that he was convinced that a strait existed which would lead into the Indian Ocean, past the New World of Amerigo, and that the Spice Islands were beyond the line of demarcation and within the Spanish sphere of influence. There is some evidence that Spanish merchant vessels, trading secretly to obtain Brazil wood, had already caught sight of the strait afterwards named after Magelhaens, and certainly such a strait is represented upon Schoner's globes dated 1515 and 1520—earlier than Magelhaens' discovery. The Portuguese were fully aware of the dangers threatened to their monopoly of the spice trade—which by this time had been firmly established—owing to the presence of Serrao in Ternate, and did all in their power to dissuade Charles from sending out the threatened expedition, pointing out that they would consider it an unfriendly act if such an expedition were permitted to start. Notwithstanding this the Emperor persisted in the project, and on Tuesday, 20th September 1519, a fleet of five vessels, the *Trinidad, St. Antonio, Concepcion, Victoria,* and *St. Jago,* manned by a heterogeneous collection of Spaniards, Portuguese, Basques, Genoese, Sicilians, French, Flemings, Germans, Greeks, Neapolitans, Corfiotes, Negroes, Malays, and a single Englishman (Master Andrew of Bristol), started from Seville upon perhaps the most important voyage of discovery ever made. So great was the antipathy between Spanish and Portuguese that disaffection broke out almost from the start, and after the mouth of the La Plata had been carefully explored, to ascertain whether this was not really the beginning of a passage through the New World, a mutiny broke out on the 2nd April 1520, in Port St. Julian, where it had been determined to winter; for of course by this time the sailors had become aware that the time of the seasons was reversed in the Southern Hemisphere. Magelhaens showed great firmness and skill in dealing with the mutiny; its chief leaders were either executed or marooned, and on the 18th October he resumed his voyage. Meanwhile the habits and customs of the natives had been observed—their huge height and uncouth foot-coverings, for which Magelhaens gave them the name of Patagonians. Within three days they had arrived at the entrance of the passage which still bears Magelhaens' name. By this time one of the ships, the *St Jago*, had been lost, and it was with only four of his vessels—the *Trinidad*, the *Victoria*, the *Concepcion*. and

the *St. Antonio*—that, Magelhaens
FERDINAND MAGELLAN. began his passage. There are many twists and divisions in the strait, and on arriving at one of the partings, Magelhaens despatched the *St. Antonio* to explore it, while he proceeded with the other three ships along the more direct route. The pilot of the *St. Antonio* had been one of the mutineers, and persuaded the crew to seize this opportunity to turn back altogether; so that when Magelhaens arrived at the appointed place of junction, no news could be ascertained of the missing vessel; it went straight back to Portugal. Magelhaens determined to continue his search, even, he said, if it came to eating the leather thongs of the sails. It had taken him thirty-eight days to get through the Straits, and for four months afterwards Magelhaens continued his course through the ocean, which, from its calmness, he called Pacific; taking a north-westerly course, and thus, by a curious chance, only hitting upon a couple of small uninhabited islands throughout their whole voyage, through a sea which we now know to be dotted by innumerable inhabited islands. On the 6th March 1520 they had sighted the Ladrones, and obtained much-needed provisions. Scurvy had broken out in its severest form, and the only Englishman on the ships died at the Ladrones. From there they went on to the islands now known as the Philippines, one of the kings of which greeted them very favourably. As a reward Magelhaens undertook one of his local quarrels, and fell in an unequal fight at Mactan, 27th April 1521. The three vessels continued their course for the Moluccas, but the *Concepcion* proved so unseaworthy that they had to beach and burn her. They reached Borneo, and here Juan Sebastian del Cano was appointed captain of the *Victoria*.

At last, on the 6th November 1521, they reached the goal of their journey, and anchored at Tidor, one of the Moluccas. They traded on very advantageous terms with the natives, and filled their holds with the spices and nutmegs for which they had journeyed so far; but when they attempted to resume their journey homeward, it was found that the *Trinidad* was too unseaworthy to proceed at once, and it was decided that the *Victoria* should start so as to get the east monsoon. This she did, and after the usual journey round the Cape of Good Hope, arrived off the Mole of Seville on Monday the 8th September 1522—three years all but twelve days from the date of their departure from Spain. Of the two hundred and seventy men who had started with the fleet, only eighteen returned in the *Victoria*. According to the ship's reckoning they had arrived on Sunday the 7th, and for some time it was a puzzle to account for the day thus lost.

Meanwhile the *Trinidad*, which had been left behind at the Moluccas, had attempted to sail back to Panama, and reached as far north as 43°, somewhere about longitude 175° W. Here provisions failed them, and they had to return to the Moluccas, where they were seized, practically as pirates, by a fleet of Portuguese vessels sent specially to prevent interference by the Spaniards with the Portuguese monopoly of the spice trade. The crew of the *Trinidad* were seized and made prisoners, and ultimately only four of them reached Spain again, after many adventures. Thirteen others, who had landed at the Cape de Verde Islands from the *Victoria*, may also be included among the survivors of the fleet, so that a total number of thirty-five out of two hundred and seventy sums up the number of the first circumnavigators of the globe.

The importance of this voyage was unique when regarded from the point of view of geographical discovery. It decisively clinched the matter with regard to the existence of an entirely New World independent from Asia. In particular, the backward voyage of the *Trinidad* (which has rarely been noticed) had shown that there was a wide expanse of ocean north of the line and east of Asia, whilst the previous voyage had shown the enormous extent of sea south of the line. After the circumnavigation of the *Victoria* it was clear to cosmographers that the world was much larger than had been imagined by the ancients; or rather, perhaps one may say that Asia was smaller than had been thought by the mediæval writers. The dogged persistence shown by Magelhaens in carrying out his idea, which turned out to be a perfectly justifiable one, raises him from this point of view to a greater height than Columbus, whose month's voyage brought him exactly where he thought he would find land according to Toscanelli's map. After Magelhaens, as will be seen, the whole coast lines of the world were roughly known, except for the Arctic Circle and for Australia.

The Emperor was naturally delighted with the result of the voyage. He granted Del Cano a pension, and a coat of arms commemorating

THE WORLD ACCORDING TO PTOLEMY OF 1548.

his services. The terms of the grant are very significant: *or*, two cinnamon sticks *saltire proper*, three nutmegs and twelve cloves, a chief *gules*, a castle *or; crest*, a globe, bearing the motto, "Primus circumdedisti me" (thou wert the first to go round me); *supporters*, two Malay kings crowned, holding in the exterior hand a spice branch proper. The castle, of course, refers to Castile, but the rest of the blazon indicates the importance attributed to the voyage as resting mainly upon the visit to the Spice Islands. As we have already seen, however, the Portuguese recovered their position in the Moluccas immediately after the departure of the *Victoria*, and seven years later Charles V. gave up any claims he might possess through Magelhaens' visit.

But for a long time afterwards the Spaniards still cast longing eyes upon the Spice Islands, and the Fuggers, the great bankers of Augsburg, who financed the Spanish monarch, for a long time attempted to get possession of Peru, with the scarcely disguised object of making it a "jumping-place" from which to make a fresh attempt at obtaining possession of the Moluccas. A modern parallel will doubtless occur to the reader.

There are thus three stages to be distinguished in the successive discovery and delimitation of the New World:—

(i.) At first Columbus imagined that he had actually reached Zipangu or Japan, and achieved the object of his voyage.

(ii.) Then Amerigo Vespucci, by coasting down South America, ascertained that there was a huge unknown land intervening even between Columbus' discoveries and the long-desired Spice Islands.

- 62 -

(iii.) Magelhaens clinches this view by traversing the Southern Pacific for thousands of miles before reaching the Moluccas.

There is still a fourth stage by which it was gradually discovered that the North-west of America was not joined on to Asia, but this stage was only gradually reached and finally determined by the voyages of Behring and Cook.

[*Authorities:* Justin Winsor, *Christopher Columbus,* 1894; Guillemard, *Ferdinand Magellan,* 1894.]

CHAPTER VIII

TO THE INDIES NORTHWARD—ENGLISH, FRENCH, DUTCH, AND RUSSIAN ROUTES

The discovery of the New World had the most important consequences on the relative importance of the different nations of Europe. Hitherto the chief centres for over two thousand years had been round the shores of the Mediterranean, and, as we have seen, Venice, by her central position and extensive trade to the East, had become a world-centre during the latter Middle Ages. But after Columbus, and still more after Magelhaens, the European nations on the Atlantic were found to be closer to the New World, and, in a measure, closer to the Spice Islands, which they could reach all the way by ship, instead of having to pay expensive land freights. The trade routes through Germany became at once neglected, and it is only in the present century that she has at all recovered from the blow given to her by the discovery of the new sea routes in which she could not join. But to England, France, and the Low Countries the new outlook promised a share in the world's trade and affairs generally, which they had never hitherto possessed while the Mediterranean was the centre of commerce. If the Indies could be reached by sea, they were almost in as fortunate a position as Portugal or Spain. Almost as soon as the new routes were discovered the Northern nations attempted to utilise them, notwithstanding the Bull of Partition, which the French king laughed at, and the Protestant English and Dutch had no reason to respect. Within three years of the return of Columbus from his first voyage, Henry VII. employed John Cabot, a Venetian settled in Bristol, with his three sons, to attempt the voyage to the Indies by the North-West Passage. He appears to have re-discovered Newfoundland in 1497, and then in the following year, failing to find a passage there, coasted down North America nearly as far as Florida.

In 1534 Jacques Cartier examined the river St. Lawrence, and his discoveries were later followed up by Samuel de Champlain, who explored some of the great lakes near the St. Lawrence, and established the French rule in Canada, or Acadie, as it was then called.

Meanwhile the English had made an attempt to reach the Indies, still by a northern passage, but this time in an easterly direction. Sebastian Cabot, who had been appointed Grand Pilot of England by Edward VI., directed a voyage of exploration in 1553, under Sir Hugh Willoughby. Only one of these ships, with the pilot (Richard Chancellor) on board, survived the voyage, reaching Archangel, and then going overland to Moscow, where he was favourably received by the Czar of Russia, Ivan the Terrible. He was, however, drowned on his return, and no further attempt to reach Cathay by sea was attempted.

The North-West Passage seemed thus to promise better than that by the North-East, and in 1576 Martin Frobisher started on an exploring voyage, after having had the honour of a wave of Elizabeth's hand as he passed Greenwich. He reached Greenland, and then Labrador, and, in a subsequent voyage next year, discovered the strait named after him. His project was taken up by Sir Humphrey Gilbert, on whom, with his brother Adrian, Elizabeth conferred the privilege of making the passage to China and the Moluccas by the north-westward, north-eastward, or northward route. At the same time a patent was granted him for discovering any lands unsettled by Christian princes. A settlement was made in St. John's, Newfoundland, but on the return voyage, near the Azores, Sir Humphrey's "frigate" (a small boat of ten men), disappeared, after he had been heard to call out, "Courage, my lads; we are as near heaven by sea as by land!" This happened in 1583.

Two years after, another expedition was sent out by the merchants of London, under John Davis, who, on this and two subsequent voyages, discovered several passages trending westward, which warranted the hope of finding a northwest passage. Beside the strait named after him, it is probable that on his third voyage, in 1587, he passed through the passage now named after Hudson. His discoveries were not followed up for some twenty years, when Henry Hudson was despatched in 1607 with a crew of ten men and a boy. He reached Spitzbergen, and reached 80° N., and in the following year reached the North (Magnetic) Pole, which was then situated at 75.22° N. Two of his men were also fortunate enough to see a mermaid—probably an Eskimo woman in her *kayak*. In a third voyage, in 1609, he discovered the strait and bay which now bear his name, but was marooned by his crew, and never heard of further. He had previously, for a time, passed into the service of the Dutch, and had guided them to the river named after him, on which New York now stands. The course of English discovery in the north was for a time concluded by the voyage of William Baffin in 1615, which resulted in the discovery of the land named after him, as well as many of the islands to the north of America.

Meanwhile the Dutch had taken part in the work of discovery towards the north. They had revolted against the despotism of Philip II., who was now monarch of both Spain and Portugal. At first they attempted to adopt a route which would not bring them into collision with their old masters; and in three voyages, between 1594 and 1597, William Barentz attempted the North-East Passage, under the auspices of the States-General. He discovered Cherry Island, and touched on Spitzbergen, but failed in the main object of his search; and the attention of the Dutch was henceforth directed to seizing the Portuguese route, rather than finding a new one for themselves.

The reason they were able to do this is a curious instance of Nemesis in history. Owing to the careful series of intermarriages planned out by Ferdinand of Arragon, the Portuguese Crown and all its possessions became joined to Spain in 1580 under Philip II., just a year after the northern provinces of the Netherlands had renounced allegiance to Spain. Consequently they were free to attack not alone Spanish vessels and colonies, but also those previously belonging to Portugal. As early as 1596 Cornelius Houtman rounded the Cape and visited Sumatra and Bantam, and within fifty, years the Dutch had replaced the Portuguese in many of their Eastern possessions. In 1614 they took Malacca, and with it the command of the Spice Islands; by 1658 they had secured full possession of Ceylon. Much earlier, in 1619, they had founded Batavia in Java, which they made the centre of their East Indian possessions, as it still remains.

The English at first attempted to imitate the Dutch in their East Indian policy. The English East India Company was founded by Elizabeth in 1600, and as early as 1619 had forced the Dutch to allow them to take a third share of the profits of the Spice Islands. In order to do this several English planters settled at Amboyna, but within four years trade rivalries had reached such a pitch that the Dutch murdered some of these merchants and drove the rest from the islands. As a consequence the English Company devoted its attention to the mainland of India itself, where they soon obtained possession of Madras and Bombay, and left the islands of the Indian Ocean mainly in possession of the Dutch. We shall see later the effect of this upon the history of geography, for it was owing to their possession of the East India Islands that the Dutch were practically the discoverers of Australia. One result of the Dutch East India policy has left its traces even to the present day. In 1651 they established a colony at the Cape of Good Hope, which only fell into English hands during the Napoleonic wars, when Napoleon held Holland.

Meanwhile the English had not lost sight of the possibilities of the North-East Passage, if not for reaching the Spice Islands, at any rate as a means of tapping the overland route to China, hitherto monopolised by the Genoese. In 1558 an English gentleman, named Anthony Jenkinson, was sent as ambassador to the Czar of Muscovy, and travelled from Moscow as far as Bokhara; but he was not very fortunate in his venture, and England had to be content for some time to receive her Indian and Chinese goods from the Venetian argosies as before. But at last they saw no reason why they should not attempt direct relations with the East. A company of Levant merchants was formed in 1583 to open out direct communications with Aleppo, Bagdad, Ormuz, and Goa. They were unsuccessful at the two latter places owing to the jealousy of the Portuguese, but they made arrangements for cheaper transit of Eastern goods to England, and in 1587 the last of the Venetian argosies, a great vessel of eleven hundred tons, was wrecked off the Isle of Wight. Henceforth the English conducted their own business with the East, and Venetian and Portuguese monopoly was at an end.

But the journeys of Chancellor and Jenkinson to the Court of Moscow had more far-reaching effects; the Russians themselves were thereby led to contemplate utilising their proximity to one of the best known routes to the Far East. Shortly after Jenkinson's visit, the Czar, Ivan the Terrible, began extending his dominions eastward, sending at first a number of troops to accompany the Russian merchant Strogonof as far as the Obi in search of sables. Among the troops were a corps of six thousand Cossacks commanded by one named Vassili Yermak, who, finding the Tartars an easy prey, determined at first to set up a new kingdom for himself. In 1579 he was successful in overcoming the Tartars and their chief town Sibir, near Tobolsk; but, finding it difficult to retain his position, determined to return to his allegiance to the Czar on condition of being supported. This was readily granted, and from that time onward the Russians steadily pushed on through to the unknown country of the north of Asia, since named after the little town conquered by Yermak, of which scarcely any traces now remain. As early as 1639 they had reached the Pacific under Kupilof. A force was sent out from Yakutz, on the Lena, in 1643, which reached the Amur, and thus Russians came for the first time in contact with the Chinese, and a new method of reaching Cathay was thus obtained, while geography gained the

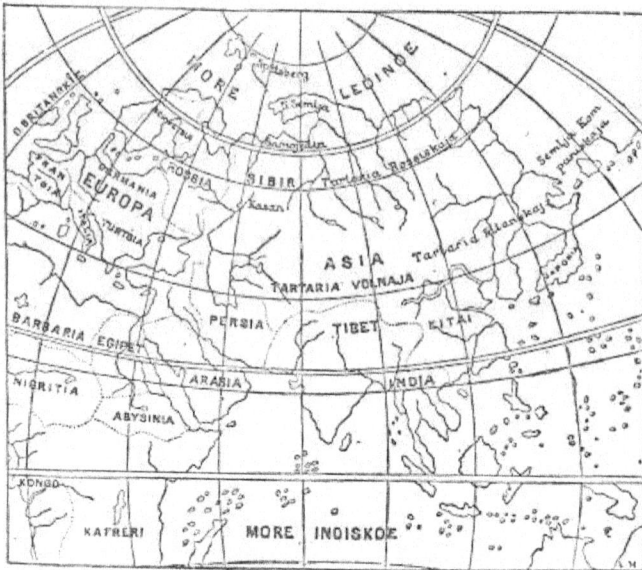

RUSSIAN MAP OF ASIA, 1737.

knowledge of the extent of Northern Asia. For, about the same time (in 1648), the Arctic Ocean was reached on the north shores of Siberia, and a fleet under the Cossack Dishinef sailed from Kolyma and reached as far as the straits known by the name of Behring. It was not, however, till fifty years afterwards, in 1696, that the Russians reached Kamtschatka.

Notwithstanding the access of knowledge which had been gained by these successive bold pushes towards north and east, it still remained uncertain whether Siberia did not join on to the northern part of the New World discovered by Columbus and Amerigo, and in 1728 Peter the Great sent out an expedition under VITUS BEHRING, a Dane in the Russian service, with the express aim of ascertaining this point. He reached Kamtschatka, and there built two vessels as directed by the Czar, and started on his voyage northward, coasting along the land. When he reached a little beyond 67° N., he found no land to the north or east, and conceived he had reached the end of the continent. As a matter of fact, he was within thirty miles of the west coast of America; but of this he does not seem to have been aware, being content with solving the special problem put before him by the Czar. The strait thus discovered by Behring, though not known by him to be a strait, has ever since been known by his name. In 1741, however, Behring again set out on a voyage of discovery to ascertain how far to the east America was, and within a fortnight had come within sight of the lofty mountain named by him Mount St. Elias. Behring himself died upon this voyage, on an island also named after him; he had at last solved the relation between the Old and the New Worlds.

These voyages of Behring, however, belong to a much later stage of discovery than those we have hitherto been treating for the last three chapters. His explorations were undertaken mainly for scientific purposes, and to solve a scientific problem, whereas all the other researches of Spanish, Portuguese, English, and Dutch were directed to one end, that of reaching the Spice Islands and Cathay. The Portuguese at first started out on the search by the slow method of creeping down the coast of Africa; the Spanish, by adopting Columbus's bold idea, had attempted it by the western route, and under Magellan's still bolder conception had equally succeeded in reaching it in that way; the English and French sought for a north-west passage to the Moluccas; while the English and Dutch attempted a northeasterly route. In both directions the icy barrier of the north prevented success. It was reserved, as we shall see, for the present century to complete the North-West Passage under Maclure, and the North-East by Nordenskiold, sailing with quite different motives to those which first brought the mariners of England, France, and Holland within the Arctic Circle.

The net result of all these attempts by the nations of Europe to wrest from the Venetians the monopoly of the Eastern trade was to add to geography the knowledge of the existence of a New World intervening between the western shores of Europe and the eastern shores of Asia. We have yet to learn the means by which the New World thus discovered became explored and possessed by the European nations.

[*Authorities:* Cooley and Beazeley, *John and Sebastian Cabot*, 1898.]

CHAPTER IX

THE PARTITION OF AMERICA

We have hitherto been dealing with the discoveries made by Spanish and Portuguese along the coast of the New World, but early in the sixteenth century they began to put foot on *terra firma* and explore the interior. As early as 1513 Vasco Nunez de Balboa ascended the highest peak in the range running from the Isthmus of Panama, and saw for the first time by European eyes the great ocean afterwards to be named by Magellan the Pacific. He there heard that the country to the south extended without end, and was inhabited by great nations, with an abundance of gold. Among his companions who heard of this golden country, or El Dorado, was one Francisco Pizarro, who was destined to test the report. But a similar report had reached the ears of Diego Velasquez, governor of Cuba, as to a great nation possessed of much gold to the north of Darien. He accordingly despatched his lieutenant Hernando Cortes in 1519 to investigate, with ten ships, six hundred and fifty men, and some eighteen horses. When he landed at the port named by him Vera Cruz, the appearance of his men, and more especially of his horses, astonished and alarmed the natives of Mexico, then a large and semi-civilised state under the rule of Montezuma, the last representative of the Aztecs, who in the twelfth century had succeeded the Toltecs, a people that had settled on the Mexican tableland as early probably as the seventh century, introducing the use of metals and roads and many of the elements of civilisation. Montezuma is reported to have been able to range no less than two hundred thousand men under his banners, but he showed his opinion of the Spaniards by sending them costly presents, gold and silver and costly stuffs. This only aroused the cupidity of Cortes, who determined to make a bold stroke for the conquest of such a rich prize. He burnt his ships and advanced into the interior of the country, conquering on his way the tribe of the Tlascalans, who had been at war with the Mexicans, but, when conquered, were ready to assist him against them. With their aid he succeeded in seizing the Mexican king, who was forced to yield a huge tribute. After many struggles Cortes found himself master of the capital, and of all the resources of the Mexican Empire (1521). These he hastened to place at the feet of the Emperor Charles V., who appointed him Governor and Captain-General of Mexico. It is characteristic throughout the history of the New World, that none of the soldiers of fortune who found it such an easy prey ever thought of setting up an empire for himself. This is a testimony to the influence national feeling had upon the minds even of the most lawless, and the result was that Europe and European ideas were brought over into America, or rather the New World became tributary to Europe.

As soon as Cortes had established himself he fitted out expeditions to explore the country, and himself reached Honduras after a remarkable journey for over 1000 miles, in which he was only guided by a map on cotton cloth, on which the Cacique of Tabasco had painted all the towns, rivers, and mountains of the country as far as Nicaragua. He also despatched a small fleet under Alvarro de Saavedra to support a Spanish expedition which had been sent to the Moluccas under Sebastian del Cano, and which arrived at Tidor in 1527, to the astonishment of Spanish and Portuguese alike when they heard he had started from New Castile. In 1536, Cortes, who had been in the meantime shorn of much of his power, conducted an expedition by sea along the north-west coast of Mexico, and reached what he considered to be a great island. He identified this with an imaginary island in the Far East, near the terrestrial paradise to which the name of California had been given in a contemporary romance. Thus, owing to Cortes, almost the whole of Central America had become known before his death in 1540. Similarly, at a much earlier period, Ponce de Leon had thought he had discovered another great island in Florida in 1512, whither he had gone in search of Bayuca, a fabled island of the Indians, in which they stated was a fountain of eternal youth. At the time of Cortes' first attempt on Mexico, Pineda had coasted round Florida, and connected it with the rest of the coast of Mexico, which he traversed as far as Vera Cruz.

The exploits of Cortes were all important in their effects. He had proved with what ease a handful of men might overcome an empire and gain unparalleled riches. Francisco Pizarro was encouraged by the success of Cortes to attempt the discovery of the El Dorado he had heard of when on Balboa's expedition. With a companion named Diego de Almegro he made several coasting expeditions down the northwest coast of South America, during which they heard of the empire of the Incas on the plateau of Peru. They also obtained sufficient gold and silver to raise their hopes of the riches of the country, and returned to Spain to report to the Emperor. Pizarro obtained permission from Charles V. to attempt the conquest of Peru, of which he was named Governor and Captain-General, on condition of paying a tribute of one-fifth of the treasure he might obtain. He started in February 1531 with a small force of 180 men, of whom thirty-six were horsemen. Adopting the policy of Cortes, he pushed directly for the capital Cuzco, where they managed to seize Atahualpa, the Inca of the time. He attempted to ransom himself by agreeing to fill the room in which he was confined, twenty-two feet long by sixteen wide, with bars of gold as high as the hand could reach. He carried out this prodigious promise, and Pizarro's companions found themselves in possession of booty equal to three millions sterling.

Atahualpa was, however, not released, but condemned to death on a frivolous pretext, while Pizarro dismissed his followers, fully confident that the wealth they carried off would attract as many men as he could desire to El Dorado. He settled himself at Lima, near the coast, in 1534. Meanwhile Almegro had been despatched south, and made himself master of Chili. Another expedition in 1539 was conducted by Pizarro's brother Gonzales across the Andes, and reached the sources of the Amazon, which one of his companions, Francisco de Orellana, traversed as far as the mouth. This he reached in August 1541, after a voyage of one thousand leagues. The river was named after Orellana, but, from reports he made of the existence of a tribe of female warriors, was afterwards known as the river of the Amazons. The author spread reports of another El Dorado to the north, in which the roofs of the temples were covered with gold. This report afterwards led to the disastrous expedition of Sir Walter Raleigh to Guiana. By his voyage Orellana connected the Spanish and Portuguese "spheres of influence" in the New World of Amerigo. By the year 1540 the main outlines of Central and South America and something of the interior had been made known by the Spanish adventurers within half a century of Columbus' first voyage. Owing to the papal bull Portugal possessed Brazil, but all the rest of the huge stretch of country was claimed for Spain. The Portuguese wisely treated Brazil as an outlet for their overflowing population, which settled there in large numbers and established plantations. The Spaniards, on the other hand, only regarded their huge possessions as exclusive markets to be merely visited by them. Rich mines of gold, silver, and mercury were discovered in Mexico and Peru, especially in the far-famed mines of Potosi, and these were exploited entirely in the interests of Spain, which acted as a sieve by which the precious metals were poured into Europe, raising prices throughout the Old World. In return European merchandise was sent in the return voyages of the Spanish galleons to New Spain, which could only buy Flemish cloth, for example, through Spanish intermediaries, who raised its price to three times the original cost. This short-sighted policy on the part of Spain naturally encouraged smuggling, and attracted the ships of all nations towards that pursuit.

We have already seen the first attempts of the French and English in the exploration of the north-east coast of North America; but during the sixteenth century very little was done to settle on such inhospitable shores, which did not offer anything like the rich prizes that Tropical America afforded. Neither the exploration of Cartier in 1534, or that of the Cabots much earlier, was followed by any attempt to possess the land. Breton fishermen visited the fisheries off Newfoundland, and various explorers attempted to find openings which would give them a north-west passage, but otherwise the more northerly part of the continent was left unoccupied till the beginning of the seventeenth century. The first town founded was that of St. Augustine, in Florida, in 1565, but this was destroyed three years later by a French expedition. Sir Walter Raleigh attempted to found a colony in 1584 near where Virginia now stands, but it failed after three years, and it was not till the reign of James I. that an organised attempt was made by England to establish plantations, as they were then called, on the North American coast.

Two Chartered Companies, the one to the north named the Plymouth Company, and the one to the south named the London Company (both founded in 1606), nominally divided between them all the coast from Nova Scotia to Florida. These large tracts of country were during the seventeenth century slowly parcelled out into smaller states, mainly Puritan in the north (New England), High Church and Catholic in the south (Virginia and Maryland). But between the two, and on the banks of the Hudson and the Delaware, two other European nations had also formed plantations—the Dutch along the Hudson from 1609 forming the New Netherlands, and the Swedes from 1636 along the Delaware forming New Sweden. The latter, however, lasted only a few years, and was absorbed by the Dutch in 1655. The capital of New Netherlands was established on Manhattan Island, to the south of the palisade still known as Wall Street, and the city was named New Amsterdam. The Hudson is such an important artery of commerce between the Atlantic and the great lakes, that this wedge between the two sets of English colonies would have been a bar to any future progress. This was recognised by Charles II., who in 1664 despatched an expedition to demand its surrender, even though England and Holland were at that time at peace. New Amsterdam was taken, and named New York, after the king's brother, the Duke of York, afterwards James II. New Sweden, which at the same time fell into the English hands, was sold as a proprietary plantation to a Jersey man, Sir George Carteret, and to a Quaker, William Penn. By this somewhat high-handed procedure the whole coast-line down to Florida was in English hands.

Both the London and Plymouth Companies had started to form plantations in 1607, and in that very year the French made their first effective settlements in America, at Port Royal and at Nova Scotia, then called Arcadie; while, the following year, Samuel de Champlain made settlements at Quebec, and founded French Canada. He explored the lake country, and established settlements down the banks of the St. Lawrence, along which French activity for a long time confined itself. Between the French and the English settlements roved the warlike Five Nations of the

Iroquois Indians, and Champlain, whose settlements were in the country of the Algonquins, was obliged to take their part and make the Iroquois the enemies of France, which had important effects upon the final struggle between England and France in the eighteenth century. The French continued their exploration of the interior of the continent. In 1673 Marquette discovered the Mississippi (Missi Sepe, "the great water"), and descended it as far as the mouth of the Arkansas, but the work of exploring the Mississippi valley was undertaken by Robert de la Salle. He had already discovered the Ohio and Illinois rivers, and in three expeditions, between 1680 and 1682, succeeded in working his way right down to the mouth of the Mississippi, giving to the huge tract of country which he had thus traversed the name of Louisiana, after Louis XIV.

France thenceforth claimed the whole *hinterland*, as we should now call it, of North America, the English being confined to the comparatively narrow strip of country east of the Alleghanies. New Orleans was founded at the mouth of the Mississippi in 1716, and named after the Prince Regent; and French activity ranged between Quebec and New Orleans, leaving many traces even to the present day, in French names like Mobile, Detroit, and the like, through the intervening country. The situation at the commencement of the eighteenth century was remarkably similar to that of the Gold Coast in Africa at the end of the nineteenth. The French persistently attempted to encroach upon the English sphere of influence, and it was in attempting to define the two spheres that George Washington learned his first lesson in diplomacy and strategy. The French and English American colonies were almost perpetually at war with one another, the objective being the spot where Pittsburg now stands, which was regarded as the gate of the west, overlooking as it did the valley of the Ohio. Here Duquesne founded the fort named after himself, and it was not till 1758 that this was finally wrested from French hands; while, in the following year, Wolfe, by his capture of Quebec, overthrew the whole French power in North America. Throughout the long fight the English had been much assisted by the guerilla warfare of the Iroquois against the French.

By the Treaty of Paris in 1763 the whole of French America was ceded to England, which also obtained possession of Florida from Spain, in exchange for the Philippines, captured during the war. As a compensation all the country west of the Mississippi became joined on to the Spanish possessions in Mexico. These of course became, nominally French when Napoleon's brother Joseph was placed on the Spanish throne, but Napoleon sold them to the United States in 1803, so that no barrier existed to the westward spread of the States. Long previously to this, a Chartered Company had been formed in 1670, with Prince Rupert at its head, to trade with the Indians for furs in Hudson's Bay, then and for some time afterwards called Rupertsland. The Hudson Bay Company gradually extended its knowledge of the northerly parts of America towards the Rocky Mountains, but it was not till 1740 that Varenne de la Varanderye discovered their extent. In 1769-71 a fur trader named Hearne traced the river Coppermine to the sea, while it was not till 1793 that Mr. (after Sir A.) Mackenzie discovered the river now named after him, and crossed the continent of North America from Atlantic to Pacific. One of the reasons for this late exploration of the north-west of North America was a geographical myth started by a Spanish voyager named Juan de Fuca as early as 1592. Coasting as far as Vancouver Island, he entered the inlet to the south of it, and not being able to see land to the north, brought back a report of a huge sea spreading over all that part of the country, which most geographers assumed to pass over into Hudson Bay or the neighbourhood. It was this report as much as anything which encouraged hopes of finding the north-west passage in a latitude low enough to be free from ice.

As soon as the United States got possession of the land west of the Mississippi they began to explore it, and between 1804 and 1807 Lewis and Clarke had explored the whole basin of the Missouri, while Pike had investigated the country between the sources of the Mississippi and the Red River. We have already seen that Behring had carried over Russian investigation and dominion into Alaska, and it was in order to avoid her encroachments down towards the Californian coast that President Monroe put forth in 1823 the doctrine that no further colonisation of the Americas would be permitted by the United States. In this year Russia agreed to limit her claims to the country north of 54.40°. The States subsequently acquired California and other adjoining states during their war with Mexico in 1848, just before gold was discovered in the Sacramento valley. The land between California and Alaska was held in joint possession between Great Britain and the States, and was known as the Oregon Territory. Lewis and Clarke had explored the Columbia River, while Vancouver had much earlier examined the island which now bears his name, so that both countries appear to have some rights of discovery to the district. At one time the inhabitants of the States were inclined to claim all the country as far as the Russian boundary 54.40°, and a war-cry arose "54.40° or fight;" but in 1846 the territory was divided by the 49th parallel, and at this date we may say the partition of America was complete, and all that remained to be known of it was the ice-bound northern coast, over which so much heroic enterprise has been displayed.

The history of geographical discovery in America is thus in large measure a history of conquest. Men got to know both coast-line and interior while endeavouring either to trade or to settle where nature was propitious, or the country afforded mineral or vegetable wealth that could be easily transported. Of the coast early knowledge was acquired for geography; but where the continent broadens out either north or south, making the interior inaccessible for trade purposes with the coasts, ignorance remained even down to the present century. Even to the present day the country south of the valley of the Amazon is perhaps as little known as any portion of the earth's surface, while, as we have seen, it was not till the early years of this century that any knowledge was acquired of the huge tract of country between the Mississippi and the Rocky Mountains. It was the natural expansion of the United States, rendered possible by the cession of this tract to the States by Napoleon in 1803, that brought it within the knowledge of all. That expansion was chiefly due to the improved methods of communication which steam has given to mankind only within this century. But for this the region east of the Rocky Mountains would possibly be as little known to Europeans, even at the present day, as the Soudan or Somaliland. It is owing to this natural expansion of the States, and in minor measure of Canada, that few great names of geographical explorers are connected with our knowledge of the interior of North America. Unknown settlers have been the pioneers of geography, and not as elsewhere has the reverse been the case. In the two other continents whose geographical history we have still to trace, Australia and Africa, explorers have preceded settlers or conquerors, and we can generally follow the course of geographical discovery in their case without the necessity of discussing their political history.

[*Authorities:* Winsor, *From Cartier to Frontenac*; Gelcich, in *Mittheilungen* of Geographical Society of Vienna, 1892.]

CHAPTER X

AUSTRALIA AND THE SOUTH SEAS—TASMAN AND COOK

If one looks at the west coast of Australia one is struck by the large number of Dutch names which are jotted down the coast. There is Hoog Island, Diemen's Bay, Houtman's Abrolhos, De Wit land, and the Archipelago of Nuyts, besides Dirk Hartog's Island and Cape Leeuwin. To the extreme north we find the Gulf of Carpentaria, and to the extreme south the island which used to be called Van Diemen's Land. It is not altogether to be wondered at that almost to the middle of this century the land we now call Australia was tolerably well known as New Holland. If the Dutch had struck the more fertile eastern shores of the Australian continent, it might have been called with reason New Holland to the present day; but there is scarcely any long coast-line of the world so inhospitable and so little promising as that of Western Australia, and one can easily understand how the Dutch, though they explored it, did not care to take possession of it.

But though the Dutch were the first to explore any considerable stretch of Australian coast, they were by no means the first to sight it. As early as 1542 a Spanish expedition under Luis Lopez de Villalobos, was despatched to follow up the discoveries of Magellan in the Pacific Ocean within the Spanish sphere of influence. He discovered several of the islands of Polynesia, and attempted to seize the Philippines, but his fleet had to return to New Spain. One of the ships coasted along an island

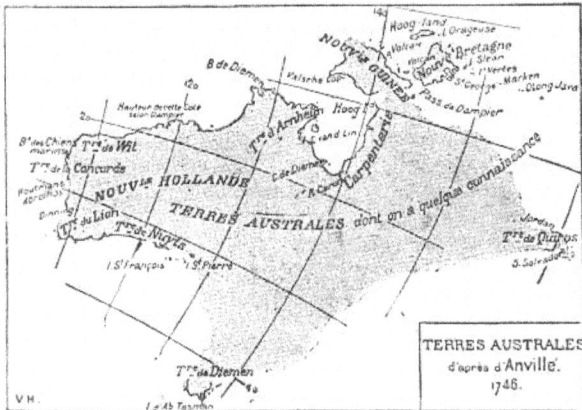

to which was given the name of New Guinea, and was thought to be part of the great unknown southern land which Ptolemy had imagined to exist in the south of the Indian Ocean, and to be connected in some way with Tierra del Fuego. Curiosity was thus aroused, and in 1606 Pedro de Quiros was despatched on a voyage to the South Seas with three ships. He discovered the New Hebrides, and believed it formed part of the southern continent, and he therefore named it Australia del Espiritu Santo, and hastened home to obtain the viceroyalty of this new possession. One of his ships got separated from him, and the commander, Luys Vaz de Torres, sailed farther to the south-west, and thereby learned that the New Australia was not a continent but an island. He proceeded farther till he came to New Guinea, which he coasted along the south coast, and seeing land to the south of him, he thus passed through the straits since named after him, and was probably the first European to see the continent of Australia. In the very same year (1606) the Dutch yacht named the *Duyfken* is said to have coasted along the south and west coasts of New Guinea nearly a thousand miles, till they reached Cape Keerweer, or "turn again." This was probably the north-west coast of Australia. In the first thirty years of the seventeenth century the Dutch followed the west coast of Australia with as much industry as the Portuguese had done with the west coast of Africa, leaving up to the present day signs of their explorations in the names of islands, bays, and capes. Dirk Hartog, in the *Endraaght*, discovered that Land which is named after his ship, and the cape and roadstead named after himself, in 1616. Jan Edels left his name upon the western coast in 1619; while, three years later, a ship named the *Lioness* or *Leeuwin* reached the most western point of the continent, to which its name is still attached.

Five years later, in 1627, De Nuyts coasted round the south coast of Australia; while in the same year a Dutch commander named Carpenter discovered and gave his name to the immense indentation still known as the Gulf of Carpentaria.

But still more important discoveries were made in 1642 by an expedition sent out from Batavia under ABEL JANSSEN TASMAN to investigate the real extent of the southern land. After the voyages of the *Leeuwin* and De Nuyts it was seen that the southern coast of the new land trended to the east, instead of working round to the west, as would have been the case if Ptolemy's views had been correct. Tasman's problem was to discover whether it was connected with the great southern land assumed to lie to the south of South America. Tasman first sailed from Mauritius, and then directing his course to the south-east, going much more south than Cape Leeuwin, at last reached land in latitude 43.30° and longitude 163.50°. This he called Van Diemen's Land, after the name of the Governor-General of Batavia, and it was assumed that this joined on to the land already discovered by De Nuyts. Sailing farther to the eastward, Tasman came out into the open sea again, and thus appeared to prove that the newly discovered land was not connected with the great unknown continent round the south pole.

But he soon came across land which might possibly answer to that description, and he called it Staaten Land, in honour of the States-General of the Netherlands. This was undoubtedly some part of New Zealand. Still steering eastward, but with a more northerly trend, Tasman discovered several islands in the Pacific, and ultimately reached Batavia after touching on New Guinea. His discoveries were a great advance on previous knowledge; he had at any rate reduced the possible dimensions of the unknown continent of the south within narrow limits, and his discoveries were justly inscribed upon the map of the world cut in stone upon the new Staathaus in Amsterdam, in which the name New Holland was given by order of the States-General to the western part of the "terra Australis." When England for a time became joined on to Holland under the rule of William III., William Dampier was despatched to New Holland to make further discoveries. He retraced the explorations of the Dutch from Dirk Hartog's Bay to New Guinea, and appears to have been the first European to have noticed the habits of the kangaroo; otherwise his voyage did not add much to geographical knowledge, though when he left the coasts of New Guinea he steered between New England and New Ireland.

As a result of these Dutch voyages the existence of a great land somewhere to the south-east of Asia became common property to all civilised men. As an instance of this familiarity many years before Cook's epoch-making voyages, it may be mentioned that in 1699 Captain Lemuel Gulliver (in Swift's celebrated romance) arrived at the kingdom of Lilliput by steering north-west from Van Diemen's Land, which he mentions by name. Lilliput, it would thus appear, was situated somewhere in the neighbourhood of the great Bight of Australia. This curious mixture of definite knowledge and vague ignorance on the part of Swift exactly corresponds to the state of geographical knowledge about Australia in his days, as is shown in the preceding map of those parts of the world, as given by the great French cartographer D'Anville in 1745 (p. 157).

These discoveries of the Spanish and Dutch were direct results and corollaries of the great search for the Spice Islands, which has formed the main subject of our inquiries. The discoveries were mostly made by ships fitted out in the Malay archipelago, if not from the Spice Islands themselves. But at the beginning of the eighteenth century new motives came into play in the search for new lands; by that time almost the whole coast-line of the world was roughly known. The Portuguese had coasted Africa, the Spanish South America, the English most of the east of North America, while Central America was known through the Spaniards. Many of the islands of the Pacific Ocean had been touched upon, though not accurately surveyed, and there remained only the north-west coast of America and the north-east coast of Asia to be explored, while the great remaining problem of geography was to discover if the great southern continent assumed by Ptolemy existed, and, if so, what were its dimensions. It happened that all these problems of coastline geography, if we may so call it, were destined to be solved by one man, an Englishman named JAMES COOK, who, with Prince Henry, Magellan, and Tasman, may be said to have determined the limits of the habitable land.

His voyages were made in the interests, not of trade or conquest, but of scientific curiosity; and they were, appropriately enough, begun in the interests of quite a different science than that of geography. The English astronomer Halley had left as a sort of legacy the task of examining the transit of Venus, which he predicted for the year 1769, pointing out its paramount importance for determining the distance of the sun from the earth. This transit could only be observed in the southern hemisphere, and it was in order to observe it that Cook made his first voyage of exploration.

There was a double suitability in the motive of Cook's first voyage. The work of his life could only have been carried out owing to the improvement in nautical instruments which had been made during the early part of the eighteenth century. Hadley had invented the sextant, by which the sun's elevation could be taken with much more ease and accuracy than with the old cross-staff, the very rough gnomon which the earlier navigators had to use. Still more important for scientific geography was the improvement that had taken place in accurate chronometry. To find the latitude of a place is not so difficult—the length of the day at different times of the year will by itself be almost enough to determine this, as we have seen in the very earliest history of Greek geography—but to determine the longitude was a much more difficult task, which in the earlier stages could only be formed by guesswork and dead reckonings.

But when clocks had been brought to such a pitch of accuracy that they would not lose but a few seconds or minutes during the whole voyage, they could be used to determine the difference of local time between any spot on the earth's surface and that of the port from which the ship sailed, or from some fixed place where the clock could be timed. The English government, seeing the importance of this, proposed the very large reward of £10,000 for the invention of a chronometer which would not lose more than a stated number of minutes during a year. This prize was won by John Harrison, and from this time onward a sea-captain with a minimum of astronomical knowledge was enabled to know his longitude within a few minutes. Hadley's sextant and Harrison's chronometer were the necessary implements to enable James Cook to do his work, which was thus, both in aim and method, in every way English.

James Cook was a practical sailor, who had shown considerable intelligence in sounding the St. Lawrence on Wolfe's expedition, and had afterwards been appointed marine surveyor of Newfoundland. When the Royal Society determined to send out an expedition to observe the transit of Venus, according to Halley's prediction, they were deterred from entrusting the expedition to a scientific man by the example of Halley himself, who had failed to obtain obedience from sailors on being entrusted with the command. Dalrymple, the chief hydrographer of the Admiralty, who had chief claims to the command, was also somewhat of a faddist, and Cook was selected almost as a *dernier ressort*. The choice proved an excellent one. He selected a coasting coaler named the *Endeavour*, of 360 tons, because her breadth of beam would enable her to carry more stores and to run near coasts. Just before they started Captain Wallis returned from a voyage round the world upon which he had discovered or re-discovered Tahiti, and he recommended this as a suitable place for observing the transit.

Cook duly arrived there, and on the 3rd of June 1769 the main object of the expedition was fulfilled by a successful observation. But he then proceeded farther, and arrived soon at a land which he saw reason to identify with the Staaten Land of Tasman; but on coasting along this, Cook found that, so far from belonging to a great southern continent, it was composed of two islands, between which he sailed, giving his name to the strait separating them. Leaving New Zealand on the 31st of March 1770, on the 20th of the next month he came across another land to the westward, hitherto unknown to mariners. Entering an inlet, he explored the neighbourhood with the aid of Mr. Joseph Banks, the naturalist of the expedition. He found so many plants new to him, that the bay was termed Botany Bay.

He then coasted northward, and nearly lost his ship upon the great reef running down the eastern coast; but by keeping within it he managed to reach the extreme end of the land in this direction, and proved that it was distinct from New Guinea. In other words, he had reached the southern point of the strait named after Torres. To this immense line of coast Cook gave the name of New South Wales, from some resemblance that he saw to the coast about Swansea. By this first voyage Cook had proved that neither New Holland nor Staaten Land belonged to the great Antarctic continent, which remained the sole myth bequeathed by the ancients which had not yet been definitely removed from the maps. In his second voyage, starting in 1772, he was directed to settle finally this problem. He went at once to the Cape of Good Hope, and from there started out on a zigzag journey round the Southern Pole, poking the nose of his vessel in all directions as far south as he could reach, only pulling up when he touched ice. In whatever direction he advanced he failed to find any trace of extensive land corresponding to the supposed Antarctic continent, which he thus definitely proved to be non-existent. He spent the remainder of this voyage in rediscovering various sets of archipelagos which preceding Spanish, Dutch, and English navigators had touched, but had never accurately surveyed. Later on Cook made a run across the Pacific from New Zealand to Cape Horn without discovering any extensive land, thus clinching the matter after three years' careful inquiry. It is worthy of remark that during that long time he lost but four out of 118 men, and only one of them by sickness.

Only one great problem to maritime geography still remained to be solved, that of the north-west passage, which, as we have seen, had so frequently been tried by English navigators, working from the east through Hudson's Bay. In 1776 Cook was deputed by George III. to attempt the solution of this problem by a new method. He was directed to endeavour to find an opening on the north-west coast of America which would lead into Hudson's Bay. The old legend of Juan de Fuca's great bay still misled geographers as to this coast. Cook not alone settled this problem, but, by advancing through Behring Strait and examining both sides of it, determined that the two continents of Asia and America approached one another as near as thirty-six miles. On his return voyage he landed at Owhyee (Hawaii), where he was slain in 1777, and his ships returned to England without adding anything further to geographical knowledge.

Cook's voyages had aroused the generous emulation of the French, who, to their eternal honour, had given directions to their fleet to respect his vessels wherever found, though France was at that time at war with England. In 1783 an expedition was sent, under François de la Pérouse, to complete Cook's work. He explored the north-east coast of Asia, examined the island of Saghalien, and passed through the strait between it and Japan, often called by his name. In Kamtschatka La Pérouse landed Monsieur Lesseps, who had accompanied the expedition as Russian interpreter, and sent home by him his journals and surveys. Lesseps made a careful examination of Kamtschatka himself, and succeeded in passing overland thence to Paris, being the first European to journey completely across the Old World from the Pacific to the Atlantic Ocean. La Pérouse then proceeded to follow Cook by examining the coast of New South Wales, and to his surprise, when entering a fine harbour in the middle of the coast, found there English ships engaged in settling the first Australian colony in 1787. After again delivering his surveys to be forwarded by the Englishmen, he started to survey the coast of New Holland, but his expedition was never heard of afterwards. As late as 1826 it was discovered that they had been wrecked on Vanikoro, an island near the Fijis.

We have seen that Cook's exploration of the eastern coast of Australia was soon followed up by a settlement. A number of convicts were sent out under Captain Philips to Botany Bay, and from that time onward English explorers gradually determined with accuracy both the coast-line and the interior of the huge stretch of land known to us as Australia. One of the ships that had accompanied Cook on his second voyage had made a rough survey of Van Diemen's Land, and had come to the conclusion that it joined on to the mainland. But in 1797, Bass, a surgeon in the navy, coasted down from Port Jackson to the south in a fine whale boat with a crew of six men, and discovered open sea running between the southernmost point and Van Diemen's Land; this is still known as Bass' Strait. A companion of his, named Flinders, coasted, in 1799, along the south coast from Cape Leeuwin eastward, and on this voyage met a French ship at Encounter Bay, so named from the *rencontre*. Proceeding farther, he discovered Port Philip; and the coast-line of Australia was approximately settled after Captain P. P. King in four voyages, between 1817 and 1822, had investigated the river mouths.

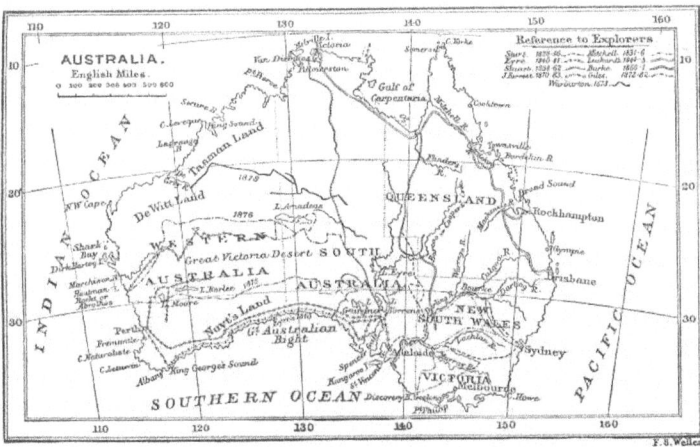

THE EXPLORATION OF AUSTRALIA.

The interior now remained to be investigated. On the east coast this was rendered difficult by the range of the Blue Mountains, honeycombed throughout with huge gullies, which led investigators time after time into a cul-de-sac; but in 1813 Philip Wentworth managed to cross them, and found a fertile plateau to the westward. Next year Evans discovered the Lachlan and Macquarie rivers, and penetrated farther into the Bathurst plains. In 1828-29 Captain Sturt increased the knowledge of the interior by tracing the course of the two great rivers Darling and Murray. In 1848 the German explorer Leichhardt lost his life in an attempt to penetrate the interior northward; but in 1860 two explorers, named Burke and Wills, managed to pass from south to north along the east coast; while, in the four years 1858 to 1862, John M'Dowall Stuart performed the still more difficult feat of crossing the centre of the continent from south to north, in order to trace a course for the telegraphic line which was shortly afterwards erected. By this time settlements had sprung up throughout the whole coast of Eastern Australia, and there only remained the western desert to be explored. This was effected in two journeys of John Forrest, between 1868 and 1874, who penetrated from Western Australia as far as the central telegraphic line; while, between 1872 and 1876, Ernest Giles performed the same feat to the north. Quite recently, in 1897, these two routes were joined by the journey of the Honourable Daniel Carnegie from the Coolgardie gold fields in the south to those of Kimberley in the north. These explorations, while adding to our knowledge of the interior of Australia, have only confirmed the impression that it was not worth knowing.

[*Authorities:* Rev. G. Grimm, *Discovsry and Exploration of Australia* (Melbourne, 1888); A. F. Calvert, *Discovery of Australia*, 1893; *Exploration of Australia*, 1895; *Early Voyages to Australia*, Hakluyt Society.]

CHAPTER XI

EXPLORATION AND PARTITION OF AFRICA: PARK—LIVINGSTONE—STANLEY

We have seen how the Portuguese had slowly coasted along the shore of Africa during the fifteeenth century in search of a way to the Indies. By the end of the century mariners *portulanos* gave a rude yet effective account of the littoral of Africa, both on the west and the eastern side. Not alone did they explore the coast, but they settled upon it. At Amina on the Guinea coast, at Loando near the Congo, and at Benguela on the western coast, they established stations whence to despatch the gold and ivory, and, above all, the slaves, which turned out to be the chief African products of use to Europeans. On the east coast they settled at Sofala, a port of Mozambique; and in Zanzibar they possessed no less than three ports, those first visited by Vasco da Gama and afterwards celebrated by Milton in the sonorous line contained in the gorgeous geographical excursus in the Eleventh Book—

> "Mombaza and Quiloa and Melind."
> —*Paradise Lost*, xi. 339.

It is probable that, besides settling on the coast, the Portuguese from time to time made explorations into the interior. At any rate, in some maps of the sixteenth and seventeenth century there is shown a remarkable knowledge of the course of the Nile. We get it terminated in three large lakes, which can be scarcely other than the Victoria and Albert Nyanza, and Tanganyika. The Mountains of the Moon also figure prominently, and it was only almost the other day that Mr. Stanley re-discovered them. It is difficult, however, to determine how far these entries on the Portuguese maps were due to actual knowledge or report, or to the traditions of a still earlier knowledge of these lakes and mountains; for in the maps accompanying the early editions of Ptolemy we likewise obtain the same information, which is repeated by the Arabic geographers, obviously from Ptolemy, and not from actual observation. When the two great French cartographers Delisle and D'Anville determined not to insert anything on their maps for which they had not some evidence, these lakes and mountains disappeared, and thus it has come about that maps of the seventeenth century often appear to display more knowledge of the interior of Africa than those of the beginning of the nineteenth, at least with regard to the sources of the Nile.

African exploration of the interior begins with the search for the sources of the Nile, and has been mainly concluded by the determination of the course of the three other great rivers, the Niger, the Zambesi, and the Congo. It is remarkable that all four rivers have had their course determined by persons of British nationality. The names of Bruce and Grant will always be associated with the Nile, that of Mungo Park with the Niger, Dr. Livingstone with the Zambesi, and Mr. Stanley with

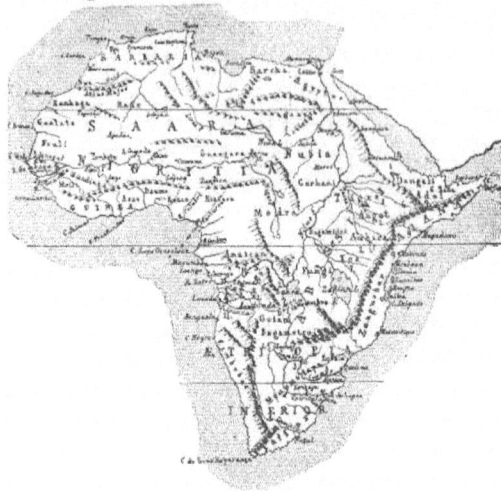

DAPPER'S MAP OF AFRICA, 1676.

the Congo. It is not inappropriate that, except in the case of the Congo, England should control the course of the rivers which her sons first made accessible to civilisation.

We have seen that there was an ancient tradition reported by Herodotus, that the Nile trended off to the west and became there the river Niger; while still earlier there was an impression that part of it at any rate wandered eastward, and some way joined on to the same source as the Tigris and Euphrates—at least that seems to be the suggestion in the biblical account of Paradise. Whatever the reason, the greatest uncertainty existed as to the actual course of the river, and to discover the source of the Nile was for many centuries the standing expression for performing the impossible. In 1768, James Bruce, a Scottish gentleman of position, set out with the determination of solving this mystery—a determination which he had made in early youth, and carried out with characteristic pertinacity. He had acquired a certain amount of knowledge of Arabic and acquaintance with African customs as Consul at Algiers. He went up the Nile as far as Farsunt, and then crossed the desert to the Red Sea, went over to Jedda, from which he took ship for Massowah, and began his search for the sources of the Nile in Abyssinia. He visited the ruins of Axum, the former capital, and in the neighbourhood of that place saw the incident with which his travels have always been associated, in which a couple of rump-steaks were extracted from a cow while alive, the wound sewn up, and the animal driven on farther.

Here, guided by some Gallas, he worked his way up the Blue Nile to the three fountains, which he declared to be the true sources of the Nile, and identified with the three mysterious lakes in the old maps. From there he worked his way down the Nile, reaching Cairo in 1773. Of course what he had discovered was merely the source of the Blue Nile, and even this had been previously visited by a Portuguese traveller named Payz. But the interesting adventures which he experienced, and the interesting style in which he told them, aroused universal attention, which was perhaps increased by the fact that his journey was undertaken purely from love of adventure and discovery. The year 1768 is distinguished by the two journeys of James Cook and James Bruce, both of them expressly for purposes of geographical discovery, and thus inaugurating the era of what may be called scientific exploration. Ten years later an association was formed named the African Association, expressly intended to explore the unknown parts of Africa, and the first geographical society called into existence. In 1795 MUNGO PARK was despatched by the Association to the west coast. He started from the Gambia, and after many adventures, in which he was captured by the Moors, arrived at the banks of the Niger, which he traced along its middle course, but failed to reach as far as Timbuctoo. He made a second attempt in 1805, hoping by sailing down the Niger to prove its identity with the river known at its mouth as the Congo; but he was forced to return, and died at Boussa, without having determined the remaining course of the Niger.

Attention was thus drawn to the existence of the mysterious city of Timbuctoo, of which Mungo Park had brought back curious rumours on his return from his first journey. This was visited in 1811 by a British seaman named Adams, who had been wrecked on the Moorish coast, and taken as a slave by the Moors across to Timbuctoo. He was ultimately ransomed by the British consul at Mogador, and his account revived interest in West African exploration. Attempts were made to penetrate the secret of the Niger, both from Senegambia and from the Congo, but both were failures, and a fresh method was adopted, possibly owing to Adams' experience in the attempt to reach the Niger by the caravan routes across the Sahara. In 1822 Major Denham and Lieutenant Clapperton left Murzouk, the capital of Fezzan, and made their way to Lake Chad and thence to Bornu. Clapperton, later on, again visited the Niger from Benin. Altogether these two travellers added some two thousand miles of route to our knowledge of, West Africa. In 1826-27 Timbuctoo was at last visited by two Europeans—Major Laing in the former year, who was murdered there; and a young Frenchman, René Caillié, in the latter. His account aroused great interest, and Tennyson began his poetic career by a prize-poem on the subject of the mysterious African capital.

It was not till 1850 that the work of Denham and Clapperton was again taken up by Barth, who for five years explored the whole country to the west of Lake Chad, visiting Timbuctoo, and connecting the lines of route of Clapperton and Caillié. What he did for the west of Lake Chad was accomplished by Nachtigall east of that lake in Darfur and Wadai, in a journey which likewise took five years (1869-74). Of recent years political interests have caused numerous expeditions, especially by the French to connect their possessions in Algeria and Tunis with those on the Gold Coast and on the Senegal.

The next stage in African exploration is connected with the name of the man to whom can be traced practically the whole of recent discoveries. By his tact in dealing with the natives, by his calm pertinacity and dauntless courage, DAVID LIVINGSTONE succeeded in opening up the entirely unknown districts of Central Africa. Starting from the Cape in 1849, he worked his way northward to the Zambesi, and then to Lake Dilolo, and after five years' wandering reached the western coast of Africa at Loanda. Then retracing his steps to the Zambesi again, he followed its course to its mouth on the east coast, thus for the first time crossing Africa from west to east. In a second journey, on which he started in 1858, he commenced tracing the course of the river Shiré, the most important affluent of the Zambesi, and in so doing arrived on the shores of Lake Nyassa in September 1859.

Meanwhile two explorers, Captain (afterwards Sir Richard) Burton and Captain Speke, had started from Zanzibar to discover a lake of which rumours had for a long time been heard, and in the following year succeeded in reaching Lake Tanganyika. On their return Speke parted from Burton and took a route more to the north, from which he saw another great lake, which afterwards turned out to be the Victoria Nyanza. In 1860, with another companion (Captain Grant), Speke returned to the Victoria Nyanza, and traced out its course. On the north of it they found a great river trending to the north, which they followed as far as Gondokoro. Here they found Mr. (afterwards Sir Samuel) Baker, who had travelled up the White Nile to investigate its source, which they thus proved to be in the Lake Victoria Nyanza. Baker continued his search, and succeeded in showing that another source of the Nile was to be found in a smaller lake to the west, which he named Albert Nyanza. Thus these three Englishmen had combined to solve the long-sought problem of the sources of the Nile.

The discoveries of the Englishmen were soon followed up by important political action by the Khedive of Egypt, Ismail Pasha, who claimed the whole course of the Nile as part of his dominions, and established stations all along it. This, of course, led to full information about the basin of the Nile being acquired for geographical purposes, and, under Sir Samuel Baker and Colonel Gordon, civilisation was for a time in possession of the Nile from its source to its mouth.

Meanwhile Livingstone had set himself to solve the problem of the great Lake Tanganyika, and started on his last journey in 1865 for that purpose. He discovered Lakes Moero and Bangweolo, and the river Nyangoue, also known as Lualaba. So much interest had been aroused by Livingstone's previous exploits of discovery, that when nothing had been heard of him for some time, in 1869 Mr. H. M. Stanley was sent by the proprietors of the *New York Herald*, for whom he had previously acted as war-correspondent, to find Livingstone. He started in 1871 from Zanzibar, and before the end of the year had come across a white man in the heart of the Dark Continent, and greeted him with the historic query, "Dr. Livingstone, I presume?" Two years later Livingstone died, a martyr to geographical and missionary enthusiasm. His work was taken up by Mr. Stanley, who in 1876 was again despatched to continue Livingstone's work, and succeeded in crossing the Dark Continent from Zanzibar to the mouth of the Congo, the whole course of which he traced, proving that the Lualaba or Nyangoue were merely different names or affluents of this mighty stream. Stanley's remarkable journey completed the rough outline of African geography by defining the course of the fourth great river of the continent.

But Stanley's journey across the Dark Continent was destined to be the starting-point of an entirely new development of the African problem. Even while Stanley was on his journey a conference had been assembled at Brussels by King Leopold, in which an international committee was formed representing all the nations of Europe, nominally for the exploration of Africa, but, as it turned out, really for its partition among the European powers. Within fifteen years of the assembly of the conference the interior of Africa had been parcelled out, mainly among the five powers, England, France, Germany, Portugal, and Belgium. As in the case of America, geographical discovery was soon followed by political division.

EXPLORATION AND PARTITION OF AFRICA.

The process began by the carving out of a state covering the whole of the newly-discovered Congo, nominally independent, but really forming a colony of Belgium, King Leopold supplying the funds for that purpose. Mr. Stanley was despatched in 1879 to establish stations along the lower course of the river, but, to his surprise, he found that he had been anticipated by M. de Brazza, a Portuguese in the service of France, who had been despatched on a secret mission to anticipate the King of the Belgians in seizing the important river mouth. At the same time Portugal put in claims for possession of the Congo mouth, and it became clear that international rivalries would interfere with the foundation of any state on the Congo unless some definite international arrangement was arrived at. Almost about the same time, in 1880, Germany began to enter the field as a colonising power in Africa. In South-West Africa and in the Cameroons, and somewhat later in Zanzibar, claims were set up on behalf of Germany by Prince Bismarck which conflicted with English interests in those districts, and under his presidency a Congress was held at Berlin in the winter of 1884-85 to determine the rules of the claims by which Africa could be partitioned. The old historic claims of Portugal to the coast of Africa, on which she had established stations both on the west and eastern side, were swept away by the principle that only effective occupation could furnish a claim of sovereignty. This great principle will rule henceforth the whole course of African history; in other words, the good old Border rule—

> "That they should take who have the power.
> And they should keep who can."

Almost immediately after the sitting of the Berlin Congress, and indeed during it, arrangements were come to by which the respective claims of England and Germany in South-West Africa were definitely determined. Almost immediately afterwards a similar process had to be gone through in order to determine the limits of the respective "spheres of influence," as they began to be called, of Germany and England in East Africa. A Chartered Company, called the British East Africa Association, was to administer the land north of Victoria Nyanza bounded on the west by the Congo Free State, while to the north it extended till it touched the revolted provinces of Egypt, of which we shall soon speak. In South Africa a similar Chartered Company, under the influence of Mr. Cecil Rhodes, practically controlled the whole country from Cape Colony up to German East Africa and the Congo Free State.

The winter of 1890-91 was especially productive of agreements of demarcation. After a considerable amount of friction owing to the encroachments of Major Serpa Pinto, the limits of Portuguese Angola on the west coast were then determined, being bounded on the east by the Congo Free State and British Central Africa; and at the same time Portuguese East Africa was settled in its relation both to British Central Africa on the west and German East Africa on the north. Meanwhile Italy had put in its claims for a share in the spoil, and the eastern horn of Africa, together with Abyssinia, fell to its share, though it soon had to drop it, owing to the unexpected vitality shown by the Abyssinians. In the same year (1890) agreements between Germany and England settled the line of demarcation between the Cameroons and Togoland, with the adjoining British territories; while in August of the same year an attempt was made to limit the abnormal pretensions of the French along the Niger, and as far as Lake Chad. Here the British interests were represented by another Chartered Company, the Royal Niger Company. Unfortunately the delimitation was not very definite, not being by river courses or meridians as in other cases, but merely by territories ruled over by native chiefs, whose boundaries were not then particularly distinct. This has led to considerable friction, lasting even up to the present day; and it is only with reference to the demarcation between England and France in Africa that any doubt still remains with regard to the western and central portions of the continent.

Towards the north-east the problem of delimitation had been complicated by political events, which ultimately led to another great exploring expedition by Mr. Stanley. The extension of Egypt into the Equatorial Provinces under Ismail Pasha, due in large measure to the geographical discoveries of Grant, Speke, and Baker, led to an enormous accumulation of debt, which caused the country to become bankrupt, Ismail Pasha to be deposed, and Egypt to be administered jointly by France and England on behalf of the European bondholders. This caused much dissatisfaction on the part of the Egyptian officials and army officers, who were displaced by French and English officials; and a rebellion broke out under Arabi Pasha. This led to the armed intervention of England, France having refused to co-operate, and Egypt was occupied by British troops. The Soudan and Equatorial Provinces had independently revolted under Mohammedan fanaticism, and it was determined to relinquish those Egyptian possessions, which had originally led to bankruptcy. General Gordon was despatched to relieve the various Egyptian garrisons in the south, but being without support, ultimately failed, and was killed in 1885. One of Gordon's lieutenants, a German named Schnitzler, who appears to have adopted Mohammedanism, and was known as Emin Pasha, was thus isolated in the midst of Africa near the Albert Nyanza, and Mr. Stanley was commissioned to attempt his rescue in 1887. He started to march through the Congo State, and succeeded in traversing a huge tract of forest country inhabited by diminutive savages, who probably represented the Pigmies of the ancients. He succeeded in reaching Emin Pasha, and after much persuasion induced him to accompany him to Zanzibar, only, however, to return as a German agent to the Albert Nyanza. Mr. Stanley's journey on this occasion was not without its political aspects, since he made arrangements during the eastern part of his journey for securing British influence for the lands afterwards handed over to the British East Africa Company.

All these political delimitations were naturally accompanied by explorations, partly scientific, but mainly political. Major Serpa Pinto twice crossed Africa in an attempt to connect the Portuguese settlements on the two coasts. Similarly, Lieutenant Wissmann also crossed Africa twice, between 1881 and 1887, in the interests of the Congo State, though he ultimately became an official of his native country, Germany. Captain Lugard had investigated the region between the three Lakes Nyanza, and secured it for Great Britain. In South Africa British claims were successfully and successively advanced to Bechuana-land, Mashona-land, and Matabele-land, and, under the leadership of Mr. Cecil Rhodes, a railway and telegraph were rapidly pushed forward towards the north. Owing to the enterprise of Mr. (now Sir H. H.) Johnstone, the British possessions were in 1891 pushed up as far as Nyassa-land. By that date, as we have seen, various treaties with Germany and Portugal had definitely fixed the contour lines of the different possessions of the three countries in South Africa. By 1891 the interior of Africa, which had up to 1880 been practically a blank, could be mapped out almost with as much accuracy as, at any rate, South America. Europe had taken possession of Africa.

One of the chief results of this, and formally one of its main motives, was the abolition of the slave trade. North Africa has been Mohammedan since the eighth century, and Islam has always recognised slavery, consequently the Arabs of the north have continued to make raids upon the negroes of Central Africa, to supply the Mohammedan countries of West Asia and North Africa with slaves. The Mahdist rebellion was in part at least a reaction against the abolition of slavery by Egypt, and the interest of the next few years will consist in the last stand of the slave merchants in the Soudan, in Darfur, and in Wadai, east of Lake Chad, where the only powerful independent Mohammedan Sultanate still exists. England is closely pressing upon the revolted provinces, along the upper course of the Nile; while France is attempting, by expeditions from the French Congo and through Abyssinia, to take possession of the Upper Nile before England conquers it. The race for the Upper Nile is at present one of the sources of danger of European war.

While exploration and conquest have either gone hand in hand, or succeeded one another very closely, there has been a third motive that has often led to interesting discoveries, to be followed by annexation. The mighty hunters of Africa have often brought back, not alone ivory and skins, but also interesting information of the interior. The gorgeous narratives of Gordon Cumming in the "fifties" were one of the causes which led to an interest in African exploration. Many a lad has had his imagination fired and his career determined by the exploits of Gordon Cumming, which are now, however, almost forgotten. Mr. F. C. Selous has in our time surpassed even Gordon Cumming's exploits, and has besides done excellent work as guide for the successive expeditions into South Africa.

Thus, practically within our own time, the interior of Africa, where once geographers, as the poet Butler puts it, "placed elephants instead of towns," has become known, in its main outlines, by successive series of intrepid explorers, who have often had to be warriors as well as scientific men. Whatever the motives that have led the white man into the centre of the Dark Continent—love of adventure, scientific curiosity, big game, or patriotism—the result has been that the continent has become known instead of merely its coast-line. On the whole, English exploration has been the main means by which our knowledge of the interior of Africa has been obtained, and England has been richly rewarded by coming into possession of the most promising parts of the continent—the Nile valley and temperate South Africa. But France has also gained a huge extent of country covering almost the whole of North-West Africa. While much of this is merely desert, there are caravan routes which tap the basin of the Niger and conduct its products to Algeria, conquered by France early in the century, and to Tunis, more recently appropriated. The West African provinces of France have, at any rate, this advantage, that they are nearer to the mother-country than any other colony of a European power; and the result may be that African soldiers may one of these days fight for France on European soil, just as the Indian soldiers were imported to Cyprus by Lord Beaconsfield in 1876. Meanwhile, the result of all this international ambition has been that Africa in its entirety is now known and accessible to European civilisation.

[*Authorities:* Kiepert, *Beiträgge zur Entdeckungsgeschichte Afrikas*, 1873; Brown, *The Story of Africa*, 4 vols., 1894; Scott Keltie, *The Partition of Africa*, 1896.]

CHAPTER XII

THE POLES—FRANKLIN—ROSS—NORDENSKIOLD—NANSEN

Almost the whole of the explorations which we have hitherto described or referred to had for their motive some practical purpose, whether to reach the Spice Islands or to hunt big game. Even the excursions of Davis, Frobisher, Hudson, and Baffin in pursuit of the north-west passage, and of Barentz and Chancellor in search of the north-east passage, were really in pursuit of mercantile ends. It is only with James Cook that the era of purely scientific exploration begins, though it is fair to qualify this statement by observing that the Russian expedition under Behring, already referred to, was ordered by Peter the Great to determine a strictly geographical problem, though doubtless it had its bearings on Russian ambitions. Behring and Cook between them, as we have seen, settled the problem of the relations existing between the ends of the two continents Asia and America, but what remained still to the north of *terra firma* within the Arctic Circle? That was the problem which the nineteenth century set itself to solve, and has very nearly succeeded in the solution. For the Arctic Circle we now possess maps that only show blanks over a few thousand square miles.

This knowledge has been gained by slow degrees, and by the exercise of the most heroic courage and endurance. It is a heroic tate, in which love of adventure and zeal for science have combated with and conquered the horrors of an Arctic winter, the six months' darkness in silence and desolation, the excessive cold, and the dangers of starvation. It is impossible here to go into any of the details which rendered the tale of Arctic voyages one of the most stirring in human history. All we are concerned with here is the amount of new knowledge brought back by successive expeditions within the Arctic Circle.

This region of the earth's surface is distinguished by a number of large islands in the eastern hemisphere, most of which were discovered at an early date. We have seen how the Norsemen landed and settled upon Greenland as early as the tenth century. Burrough sighted Nova Zembla in 1556; in one of the voyages in search of the north-east passage, though the very name (Russian for Newfoundland) implies that it had previously been sighted and named by Russian seamen. Barentz is credited with having sighted Spitzbergen. The numerous islands to the north of Siberia became known through the Russian investigations of Discheneff, Behring, and their followers; while the intricate network of islands to the north of the continent of North America had been slowly worked out during the search for the north-west passage. It was indeed in pursuit of this will-of-the-wisp that most of the discoveries in the Arctic Circle were made, and a general impetus given to Arctic exploration.

It is with a renewed attempt after this search that the modern history of Arctic exploration begins. In 1818 two expeditions were sent under the influence of Sir Joseph Banks to search the north-west passage, and to attempt to reach the Pole. The former was the objective of John Ross in the *Isabella* and W. E. Parry in the *Alexander*, while in the Polar exploration John Franklin sailed in the *Trent*. Both expeditions were unsuccessful, though Ross and Parry confirmed Baffin's discoveries. Notwithstanding this, two expeditions were sent two years later to attempt the north-west passage, one by land under Franklin, and the other by sea under Parry. Parry managed to get half-way across the top of North America, discovered the archipelago named after him, and reached 114° West longitude, thereby gaining the prize of £5000 given by the British Parliament for the first seaman that sailed west of the 110th meridian. He was brought up, however, by Banks Land, while the strait which, if he had known it, would have enabled him to complete the north-west passage, was at that time closed by ice. In two successive voyages, in 1822 and 1824, Parry increased the detailed knowledge of the coasts he had already discovered, but failed to reach even as far westward as he had done on his first voyage. This somewhat discouraged Government attempts at exploration, and the next expedition, in 1829, was fitted out by Mr. Felix Booth, sheriff of London, who despatched the paddle steamer *Victory*, commanded by John Ross. He discovered the land known as Boothia Felix, and his nephew, James C. Ross, proved that it belonged to the mainland of America, which he coasted along by land to Cape Franklin, besides determining the exact position of the North Magnetic Pole at Cape Adelaide, on Boothia Felix. After passing five years within the Arctic Circle, Ross and his companions, who had been compelled to abandon the *Victory*, fell in with a whaler, which brought them home.

We must now revert to Franklin, who, as we have seen, had been despatched by the Admiralty to outline the north coast of America, only two points of which had been determined, the embouchures of the Coppermine and the Mackenzie, discovered respectively by Hearne and Mackenzie. It was not till 1821 that Franklin was able to start out from the mouth of the Coppermine eastward in two canoes, by which he coasted along till he came to the point named by him Point Turn-again. By that time only three days' stores of pemmican remained, and it was only with the greatest difficulty, and by subsisting on lichens and scraps of roasted leather, that they managed to return to their base of operations at Fort Enterprise. Four years later, in 1825, Franklin set out on another exploring expedition with the same object, starting this time from the mouth of the Mackenzie river, and despatching one of his companions, Richardson, to connect the coast between the Mackenzie and the Coppermine; while he himself proceeded westward to meet the Blossom, which, under Captain Beechey, had been despatched to Behring Strait to bring his party back. Richardson was entirely successful in examining the coast-line between the Mackenzie and the Coppermine; but Beechey, though he succeeded in rounding Icy Cape and tracing the coast as far as Point Barrow, did not come up to Franklin, who had only got within 160 miles at Return Reef. These 160 miles, as well as the 222 miles intervening between Cape Turn-again, Franklin's easternmost point by land, and Cape Franklin, J. C. Ross's most westerly point, were afterwards filled in by T. Simpson in 1837, after a coasting voyage in boats of 1408 miles, which stands as a record even to this day. Meanwhile the Great Fish River had been discovered and followed to its mouth by C. J. Back in 1833. During the voyage down the river, an oar broke while the boat was shooting a rapid, and one of the party commenced praying in a loud voice; whereupon the leader called out: "Is this a time for praying? Pull your starboard oar!"

Meanwhile, interest had been excited rather more towards the South Pole, and the land of which Cook had found traces in his search for the fabled Australian continent surrounding it. He had reached as far south as 71.10°, when he was brought up by the great ice barrier. In 1820-23 Weddell visited the South Shetlands, south of Cape Horn, and found an active volcano, even amidst the extreme cold of that district. He reached as far south as 74°, but failed to come across land in that district. In 1839 Bellany discovered the islands named after him, with a volcano twelve thousand feet high, and another still active on Buckle Island. In 1839 a French expedition under Dumont d'Urville again visited and explored the South Shetlands; while, in the following year, Captain Wilkes, of the United States navy, discovered the land named after him. But the most remarkable discovery made in Antarctica was that of Sir J. C. Ross, who had been sent by the Admiralty in 1840 to identify the South Magnetic Pole, as we have seen he had discovered that of the north. With the two ships *Erebus* and *Terror* he discovered Victoria Land and the two active volcanoes named after his ships, and pouring forth flaming lava, amidst the snow. In January 1842 he reached farthest south, 76°. Since his time little has been attempted in the south, though in the winter of 1894-95 C. E. Borchgrevink again visited Victoria Land.

NORTH POLAR REGION—WESTERN HALF.

On the return of the *Erebus* and *Terror* from the South Seas the government placed these two vessels at the disposal of Franklin (who had been knighted for his previous discoveries), and on the 26th of May 1845 he started with one hundred and twenty-nine souls on board the two vessels, which were provisioned up to July 1848. They were last seen by a whaler on the 26th July of the former year waiting to pass into Lancaster Sound. After penetrating as far north as 77°, through Wellington Channel, Franklin was obliged to winter upon Beechey Island, and in the following year (September 1846) his two ships were beset in Victoria Strait, about twelve miles from King William Land. Curiously enough, in the following year (1847) J. Rae had been despatched by land from Cape Repulse in Hudson's Bay, and had coasted along the east coast of Boothia, thus connecting Ross's and Franklin's coast journeys with Hudson's Bay. On 18th April 1847 Rae had reached a point on Boothia less than 150 miles from Franklin on the other side of it. Less than two months later, on the 11th June, Franklin died on the *Erebus*. His ships were only provisioned to July 1848, and remained still beset throughout the whole of 1847. Crozier, upon whom the command devolved, left the ship with one hundred and five survivors to try and reach Back's Fish River. They struggled along the west coast of King William Land, but failed to reach their destination; disease, and even starvation, gradually lessened their numbers. An old

Eskimo woman, who had watched the melancholy procession, afterwards told M'Clintock they fell down and died as they walked.

By this time considerable anxiety had been roused by the absence of any news from Franklin's party. Richardson and Rae were despatched by land in 1848, while two ships were sent on the attempt to reach Franklin through Behring Strait, and two others, the *Investigator* and the *Enterprise*, under J. C. Ross, through Baffin Bay. Rae reached the east coast of Victoria Land, and arrived within fifty miles of the spot where Franklin's two ships had been abandoned; but it was not till his second expedition by land, which started in 1853, that he obtained any news. After wintering at Lady Pelly Bay, on the 20th April 1854 Rae met a young Eskimo, who told him that four years previously forty white men had been seen dragging a boat to the south on the west shore of King William Land, and a few months later the bodies of thirty of these men had been found by the Eskimo, who produced silver with the Franklin crest to confirm the truth of their statement. Further searches by land were continued up to as late as 1879, when Lieutenant F. Schwatka, of the United States army, discovered several of the graves and skeletons of the Franklin expedition.

Neither of the two attempts by sea from the Atlantic or from the Pacific base, in 1848, having succeeded in gaining any news, the *Enterprise* and the *Investigator*, which had previously attempted to reach Franklin from the east, were despatched in 1850, under Captain R. Collinson and Captain M'Clure; to attempt the search from the west through Behring Strait. M'Clure, in the *Investigator*, did not wait for Collinson, as he had been directed, but pushed on and discovered Banks Land, and became beset in the ice in Prince of Wales Strait. In the winter of 1850-51 he endeavoured unsuccessfully to work his way from this strait into Parry Sound, but in August and September 1851 managed to coast round Banks Land to its most north-westerly point, and then succeeded in passing through the strait named after M'Clure, and reached Barrow Strait, thus performing for the first time the north-west passage, though it was not till 1853 that the *Investigator* was abandoned. Collinson, in the *Enterprise*, followed M'Clure closely, though never reaching him, and attempting to round Prince Albert Land by the south through Dolphin Strait, reached Cambridge Bay at the nearest point by ship of all the Franklin expeditions. He had to return westward, and only reached England in 1855, after an absence of five years and four months.

From the east no less than ten vessels had attempted the Franklin sea search in 1851, comprising two Admiralty expeditions, one private English one, an American combined government and private party, together with a ship put in commission by the wifely devotion of Lady Franklin. These all attempted the search of Lancaster Sound, where Franklin had last been seen, and they only succeeded in finding three graves of men who had died at an early stage, and had been buried on Beechey Island. Another set of four vessels were despatched under Sir Edward Belcher in 1852, who were fortunate enough to reach M'Clure in the *Investigator* in the following year, and enabled him to complete the north-west passage, for which he gained the reward of £10,000 offered by Parliament in 1763. But Belcher was obliged to abandon most of his vessels, one of which, the *Resolute*, drifted over a thousand miles, and having been recovered by an American whaler, was refitted by the United States and presented to the queen and people of Great Britain.

Notwithstanding all these efforts, the Franklin remains have not yet been discovered, though Dr. Rae, as we have seen, had practically ascertained their terrible fate. Lady Franklin, however, was not satisfied with this vague information. She was determined to fit out still another expedition, though already over £35,000 had been spent by private means, mostly from her own personal fortune; and in 1857 the steam yacht *Fox* was despatched under M'Clintock, who had already shown himself the most capable master of sledge work. He erected a monument to the Franklin expedition on Beechey Island in 1858, and then following Peel Sound, he made inquiries of the natives throughout the winter of 1858-59. This led him to search King William Land, where, on the 25th May, he came across a bleached human skeleton lying on its face, showing that the man had died as he walked. Meanwhile, Hobson, one of his companions, discovered a record of the Franklin expedition, stating briefly its history between 1845 and 1848; and with this definite information of the fate of the Franklin expedition M'Clintock returned to England in 1859, having succeeded in solving the problem of Franklin's fate, while exploring over 800 miles of coast-line in the neighbourhood of King William Land.

The result of the various Franklin expeditions had thus been to map out the intricate network of islands dotted over the north of North America. None of these, however, reached much farther north than 75°.

Only Smith Sound promised to lead north of the 80th parallel. This had been discovered as early as 1616 by Baffin, whose farthest north was only exceeded by forty miles, in 1852, by Inglefield in the *Isabel*, one of the ships despatched in search of Franklin. He was followed up by Kane in the *Advance*, fitted out in 1853 by the munificence of two American citizens, Grinnell and Peabody. Kane worked his way right through Smith Sound and Robeson Channel into the sea named after him. For two years he continued investigating Grinnell Land and the adjacent shores of Greenland. Subsequent investigations by Hayes in 1860, and Hall ten years later, kept alive the interest in Smith Sound and its neighbourhood; and in 1873 three ships were despatched under Captain (afterwards Sir George)

Nares, who nearly completed the survey of Grinnell Land, and one of his lieutenants, Pelham Aldrich, succeeded in reaching 82.48° N. About the same time, an Austrian expedition under Payer and Weyprecht explored the highest known land, much to the east, named by them Franz Josef Land, after the Austrian Emperor.

NORTH POLAR REGION—EASTERN HALF.

Simultaneously interest in the northern regions was aroused by the successful exploit of the north-east passage by Professor (afterwards Baron) Nordenskiold, who had made seven or eight voyages in Arctic regions between 1858 and 1870. He first established the possibility of passing from Norway to the mouth of the Yenesei in the summer, making two journeys in 1875-76. These have since been followed up for commercial purposes by Captain Wiggins, who has frequently passed from England to the mouth of the Yenesei in a merchant vessel. As Siberia develops there can be little doubt that this route will become of increasing commercial importance. Professor Nordenskiold, however, encouraged by his easy passage to the Yenesei, determined to try to get round into Behring Strait from that point, and in 1878 he started in the *Vega*, accompanied by the *Lena*, and a collier to supply them with coal. On the 19th August they passed Cape Chelyuskin, the most northerly point of the Old World. From here the *Lena* appropriately turned its course to the mouth of its namesake, while the *Vega* proceeded on her course, reaching on the 12th September

Cape North, within 120 miles of Behring Strait; this cape Cook had reached from the east in 1778. Unfortunately the ice became packed so closely that they could not proceed farther, and they had to remain in this tantalising condition for no less than ten months. On the 18th July 1879 the ice broke up, and two days later the *Vega* rounded East Cape with flying colours, saluting the easternmost coast of Asia in honour of the completion of the north-east passage. Baron Nordenskiold has since enjoyed a well-earned leisure from his arduous labours in the north by studying and publishing the history of early cartography, on which he has issued two valuable atlases, containing fac-similes of the maps and charts of the Middle Ages.

General interest thus re-aroused in Arctic exploration brought about a united effort of all the civilised nations to investigate the conditions of the Polar regions. An international Polar Conference was held at Hamburg in 1879, at which it was determined to surround the North Pole for the years 1882-83 by stations of scientific observation, intended to study the conditions of the Polar Ocean. No less than fifteen expeditions were sent forth; some to the Antarctic regions, but most of them round the North Pole. Their object was more to subserve the interest of physical geography than to promote the interest of geographical discovery; but one of the expeditions, that of the United States under Lieutenant A. W. Greely, again took up the study of Smith Sound and its outlets, and one of his men, Lieutenant Lockwood, succeeded in reaching 83.24° N., within 450 miles of the Pole, and up to that time the farthest north reached by any human being. The Greely expedition also succeeded in showing that Greenland was not so much ice-capped as ice-surrounded.

Hitherto the universal method by which discoveries had been made in the Polar regions was to establish a base at which sufficient food was cached, then to push in any required direction as far as possible, leaving successive caches to be returned to when provisions fell short on the forward journey. But in 1888, Dr. Fridjof Nansen determined on a bolder method of investigating the interior of Greenland. He was deposited upon the east coast, where there were no inhabitants, and started to cross Greenland, his life depending upon the success of his journey, since he left no reserves in the rear and it would be useless to return. He succeeded brilliantly in his attempt, and his exploit was followed up by two successive attempts of Lieutenant Peary in 1892-95, who succeeded in crossing Greenland at much higher latitude even than Nansen.

WESTERN   90 ∧   EASTERN
HEMISPHERE   HEMISPHERE

88—

NANSEN, 1895.
86—

84—
A. W. GREELY, 1882.
G. S. NARES, 1876.
W. E. PARRY, 1827.
PAYER AND WEYPRECHT,
C. F. HALL, 1870.   82—   1874.
NORDENSKIOLD, 1868.
WILLIAM SCORESBY, 1806.
J. C. PHIPPS, 1773.
E. K. KANE, 1854.   80— HUDSON, 1607.

E. A. INGLEFIELD, 1852. 78—
WILLIAM BAFFIN, 1616.   WILLIAM BARENTZ, 1594.

76—

74—
HENRY HUDSON, 1607.

JOHN DAVIS, 1587.   72—

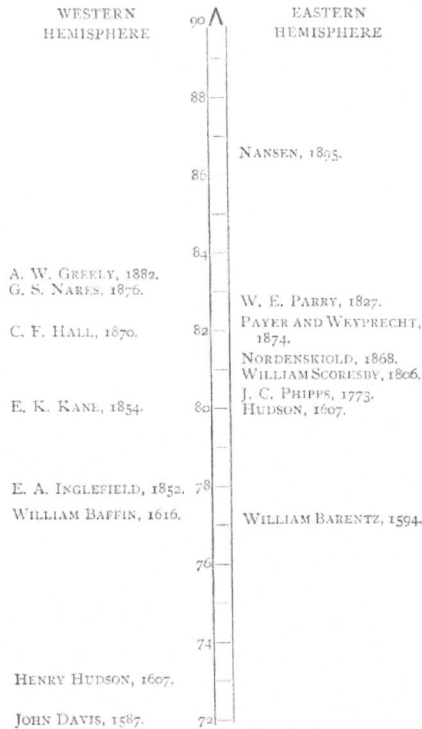

CLIMBING THE NORTH POLE

The success of his bold plan encouraged Dr. Nansen to attempt an even bolder one. He had become convinced, from the investigations conducted by the international Polar observations of 1882-83, that there was a continuous drift of the ice across the Arctic Ocean from the north-east shore of Siberia. He was confirmed in this opinion, by the fact that debris from the *Jeannette*, a ship abandoned in 1881 off the Siberian coast, drifted across to the east coast of Greenland by 1884. He had a vessel built for him, the now-renowned *Fram*, especially intended to resist the pressure of the ice. Hitherto it had been the chief aim of Arctic explorations to avoid besetment, and to try and creep round the land shores. Dr. Nansen was convinced that he could best attain his ends by boldly disregarding these canons and trusting to the drift of the ice to carry him near to the Pole. He reckoned that the drift would take some three years, and provisioned the *Fram* for five. The results of his venturous voyage confirmed in almost every particular his remarkable plan, though it was much scouted in many quarters when first announced. The drift of the ice carried him across the Polar Sea within the three years he had fixed upon for the probable duration of his journey; but finding that the drift would not carry him far enough north, he left the *Fram* with a companion, and advanced straight towards the Pole, reaching in April 1895 farthest north, 86.14°, within nearly 200 miles of the Pole. On his return journey he was lucky enough to come across Mr. F. Jackson, who in the *Windward* had established himself in 1894 in Franz Josef Land. The rencontre of the two intrepid explorers forms an apt parallel of the celebrated encounter of Stanley and Livingstone, amidst entirely opposite conditions of climate.

Nansen's voyage is for the present the final achievement of Arctic exploration, but his Greenland method of deserting his base has been followed by Andrée, who in the autumn of 1897 started in a balloon for the Pole, provisioned for a long stay in the Arctic regions. Nothing has been heard of him for the last twelve months, but after the example of Dr. Nansen there is no reason to fear just at present for his safety, and the present year may possibly see his return after a successful carrying out of one of the great aims of geographical discovery. It is curious that the attention of the world should be at the present moment directed to the Arctic regions for the two most opposite motives that can be named, lust for gold and the thirst for knowledge and honour.

[*Authorities:* Greely, *Handbook of Arctic Discoveries*, 1896.]

ANNALS OF DISCOVERY

B.C.

cir. 600. Marseilles founded.

570. Anaximander of Miletus invents maps and the gnomon.

501. Hecatæus of Miletus writes the first geography.

450. Himilco the Carthaginian said to have visited Britain.

446. Herodotus describes Egypt and Scythia.

cir. 450. Hanno the Carthaginian sails down the west coast of Africa as far as Sierra Leone.

cir. 333. Pytheas visits Britain and the Low Countries.

332. Alexander conquers Persia and visits India.

330. Nearchus sails from the Indus to the Arabian Gulf.

cir. 300. Megasthenes describes the Punjab.

cir. 200. Eratosthenes founds scientific geography.

100. Marinus of Tyre, founder of mathematical geography.

60-54. Cæsar conquers Gaul; visits Britain, Switzerland, and Germany.

20. Strabo describes the Roman Empire. First mention of Thule and Ireland.

bef. 12. Agrippa compiles a *Mappa Mundi*, the foundation of all succeeding ones.

A.D.

150. Ptolemy publishes his geography.

230. The Peutinger Table pictures the Roman roads.

400-14. Fa-hien travels through and describes Afghanistan and India.

499. Hoei-Sin said to have visited the kingdom of Fu-sang, 20,000 furlongs east of China (identified by some with California).

518-21. Hoei-Sing and Sung-Yun visit and describe the Pamirs and the Punjab.

540. Cosmas Indicopleustes visits India, and combats the sphericity of the globe.

629-46. Hiouen-Tshang travels through Turkestan, Afghanistan, India, and the Pamirs.

671-95. I-tsing travels through and describes Java, Sumatra, and India.

776. The *Mappa Mundi* of Beatus.

851-916. Suláimán and Abu Zaid visit China.

861. Naddod discovers Iceland.

884. Ibn Khordadbeh describes the trade routes between Europe and Asia.

cir. 890. Wulfstan and athere sail to the Baltic and the North Cape.

cir. 900. Gunbiörn discovers Greenland.

912-30. The geographer Mas'udi describes the lands of Islam, from Spain to Further India, in his "Meadows of Gold."

921. Ahmed Ibn Fozlan describes the Russians.

969. Ibn Haukal composes his book on Ways.

985. Eric the Red colonises Greenland.

cir. 1000. Lyef, son of Eric the Red, discovers Newfoundland (Helluland), Nova Scotia (Markland), and the mainland of North America (Vinland).

1111. Earliest use of the water-compass by Chinese.

1154. Edrisi, geographer to King Roger of Sicily, produces his geography.

1159-73. Rabbi Benjamin of Tudela visited the Persian Gulf; reported on India.

cir. 1180. The compass first mentioned by Alexander Neckam.

1255. William Ruysbroek (Rubruquis), a Fleming, visits Karakorum.

1260-71. The brothers Nicolo and Maffeo Polo, father and uncle of Marco Polo, make their first trading venture through Central Asia.

1271-95. They make their second journey, accompanied by Marco Polo; and about 1275 arrived at the Court of Kublai Khan in Shangfu, whence Marco Polo was entrusted with several missions to Cochin China, Khanbalig (Pekin), and the Indian Seas.

1280. Hereford map of Richard of Haldingham.

1284. The Ebstorf *Mappa Mundi.*

bef. 1290. The normal Portulano compiled in Barcelona.

1292. Friar John of Monte Corvino, travels in India, and afterwards becomes Archbishop of Pekin.

1325-78. Ibn Batuta, an Arab of Tangier, after performing the Mecca pilgrimage through N. Africa, visits Syria, Quiloa (E. Africa), Ormuz, S. Russia, Bulgaria, Khiva, Candahar, and attached himself to the Court of Delhi, 1334-42, whence he was despatched on an embassy to China. After his return he visited Timbuctoo.

1316-30. Odorico di Pordenone, a Minorite friar, travelled through India, by way of Persia, Bombay, and Surat, to Malabar, the Coromandel coast, and thence to China and Tibet.

1320. Flavio Gioja of Amalfi invents the compass box and card.

1312-31. Abulfeda composes his geography.

1327-72. Sir John Mandeville said to have written his travels in India.

1328. Friar Jordanus of Severac. Bishop of Quilon.

1328-49. John de Marignolli, a Franciscan friar, made a mission to China, visited Quilon in 1347, and made a pilgrimage to the shrine of St. Thomas in India in 1349.

1339. Angelico Dulcert of Majorca draws a Portulano.

1351. The Medicean Portulano compiled.

1375. Cresquez, the Jew, of Majorca, improves Dulcert's Portulano (Catalan map).

cir. 1400. Jehan Bethencourt re-discovers the Canaries.

1419. Prince Henry the Navigator establishes a geographical seminary at Sagres (died 1460).

1419-40. Nicolo Conti, a noble Venetian, travelled throughout Southern India and along the Bombay coast.

1420. Zarco discovers Madeira.

1432. Gonsalo Cabral re-discovers the Azores.

1442. Nuño Tristão reaches Cape de Verde.

1442-44. Abd-ur-Razzak, during an embassy to India, visited Calicut, Mangalore, and Vijayanagar.

1457. Fra Mauro's map.

1462. Pedro de Cintra reaches Sierra Leone.

1468-74. Athanasius Nikitin, a Russian, travelled from the Volga, through Central Asia and Persia, to Gujerat, Cambay, and Chaul, whence he proceeded inland to Bidar and Golconda.

1471. Fernando Poo discovers his island.

1471. Pedro d'Escobar crosses the line.

1474. Toscanelli's map (foundation of Behaim globe and Columbus' guide).

1478. Second printed edition of Ptolemy, with twenty-seven maps—practically the first atlas.

1484. Diego Cam discovers the Congo.

1486. Bartholomew Diaz rounds the Cape of Good Hope.

1487. Pedro de Covilham visits Ormuz, Goa, and Malabar, and afterwards settled in Abyssinia.

1492. Martin Behaim makes his globe.

1492. 6th September. Columbus starts from the Canaries.

1492. 12th October. Columbus lands at San Salvador (Watling Island).

1493. 3rd May. Bull of partition between Spain and Portugal issued by Pope Alexander VI.

1493. September. Columbus on his second voyage discovers Jamaica.

1494-99. Hieronimo di Santo Stefano, a Genoese, visited Malabar and the Coromandel coast, Ceylon and Pegu.

1497. Vasco da Gama rounds the Cape, sees Natal (Christmas Day) and Mozambique, lands at Zanzibar, and crosses to Calicut.

1497. John Cabot re-discovers Newfoundland.

1498. Columbus on his third voyage discovers Trinidad and the Orinoco.

1499. Amerigo Vespucci discovers Venezuela.

1499. Pinzon discovers mouth of Amazon, and doubles Cape St. Roque.

1500. Pedro Cabral discovers Brazil on his way to Calicut.

1500. First map of the New World, by Juan de la Cosa.

1500. Corte Real lands at mouth of St. Lawrence, and

re-discovers Labrador.

1501. Vespucci coasts down S. America and proves that it is a New World.

1501. Tristan d'Acunha discovers his island.

1501. Juan di Nova discovers the island of Ascension.

1502. Bermudez discovers his islands.

1502-4. Columbus on his fourth voyage explores Honduras.

1503-8. Travels of Ludovico di Varthema in Further India.

1505. Mascarenhas discovers the islands of Bourbon and Mauritius.

1507. Martin Waldseemüller proposes to call the New World America in his *Cosmographia*.

1509. Malacca visited by Lopes di Sequira.

1512. Molucca, or Spice Islands, visited by Francisco Serrão.

1513. Strasburg Ptolemy contains twenty new maps by Waldseemüller, forming the first modern atlas.

1513. Ponce de Leon discovers Florida.

1513. Vasco Nuñez de Balbao crosses the Isthmus of Panama, and sees the Pacific.

1517. Sebastian Cabot said to have discovered Hudson's Bay.

1517. Juan Diaz de Solis discovers the Rio de la Plata, and is murdered on the island of Martin Garcia.

1518. Grijalva discovers Mexico.

1519. Fernando Cortez conquers Mexico.

1519. Fernando Magellan starts on the circumnavigation of the globe.

1519. Guray explores north coast of Gulf of Mexico.

1520. Schoner's second globe.

1520. Magellan sees Monte Video, discovers Patagonia and Tierra del Fuego, and traverses the Pacific.

1520-26. Alvarez explores the Soudan.

1521. Magellan discovers the Ladrones (Marianas), and is killed on the Philippines.

1522. Magellan's ship *Victoria*, under Sebastian del Cano, reaches Spain, having circumnavigated the globe in three years.

1524. Verazzano, on behalf of the French King, coasts from Cape Fear to New Hampshire.

1527. Saavedra sails from west coast of Mexico to the Moluccas.

1529. Line of demarcation between Spanish and Portuguese fixed at 17° east of Moluccas.

1527. Saavedra sails from west coast of Mexico to the Moluccas.

1531. Francisco Pizarro conquers Peru.

1532. Cortez visits California.

1534. Jacques Cartier explores the gull and river of St. Lawrence.

1535. Diego d'Almagro conquers Chili.

1536. Gonsalo Pizarro passes the Andes.

1537-58. Ferdinand Mendez Pinto travels to Abyssinia, India, the Malay Archipelago, China, and Japan.

1538. Gerhardt Mercator begins his career as geographer. (Globe, 1541; projection, 1569; died 1594; atlas, 1595).

1539. Francesco de Ulloa explores the Gulf of California.

1541. Orellana sails down the Amazon.

1542. Ruy Lopez de Villalobos discovers New

Philippines, Garden Islands, and Pelew Islands, and takes possession of the Philippines for Spain.

1542. Cabrillo advances as far as Cape Mendocino.

1542. Japan first visited by Antonio de Mota.

1542. Gaetano sees the Sandwich Islands.

1543. Ortez de Retis discovers New Guinea.

1544. Sebastian Munster's *Cosmographia.*

1549. Bareto and Homera explore the lower Zambesi.

1553. Sir Hugh Willoughby attempts the North-East Passage past North Cape, and sights Novaya Zemlya.

1554. Richard Chancellor, Willoughby's pilot, reaches Archangel, and travels overland to Moscow.

1556-72. Antonio Laperis' atlas published at Rome.

1558. Anthony Jenkinson travels from Moscow to Bokhara.

1567. Alvaro Mendaña discovers Solomon Islands.

1572. Juan Fernandez discovers his island, and St. Felix and St. Ambrose Islands.

1573. Abraham Ortelius' *Teatrum Orbis Terrarum.*

1576. Martin Frobisher discovers his bay.

1577-79. Francis Drake circumnavigates the globe, and explores the west coast of North America.

1579. Yermak Timovief seizes Sibir on the Irtish.

1580. Dutch settle in Guiana.

1586. John Davis sails through his strait, and reaches lat. 72° N.

1590. Battel visits the lower Congo.

1592. The Molyneux globe.

1592. Juan de Fuca imagines he has discovered an

immense sea in the north-west of North America.

1596. William Barentz discovers Spitzbergen, and reaches lat. 80° N.

1596. Payz traverses the Horn of Africa, and visits the source of the Blue Nile.

1598. Mendaña discovers Marquesas Islands.

1598. Hakluyt publishes his *Principal Navigations.*

1599. Houtman reaches Achin, in Sumatra.

1603. Stephen Bennett re-discovers Cherry Island, 74.13° N.

1605. Louis Vaes de Torres discovers his strait.

1606. Quiros discovers Tahiti and north-east coast of Australia.

1608. Champlain discovers Lake Ontario.

1609. Henry Hudson discovers his river.

1610. Hudson passes through his strait into his bay.

1611. Jan Mayen discovers his island.

1615. Lemaire rounds Cape Horn (Hoorn), and sees New Britain.

1616. Dirk Hartog coasts West Australia to 27° S.

1616. Baffin discovers his bay.

1618. George Thompson, a Barbary merchant, sails up the Gambia.

1619. Edel and Houtman coast Western Australia to 32-1/2° S. (Edel's Land).

1622. Dutch ship *Leeuwin* reaches south-west cape of Australia.

1623. Lobo explores Abyssinia.

1627. Peter Nuyts discovers his archipelago.

1630. First meridian of longitude fixed at Ferro, in the

Canary Islands.

1631. Fox explores Hudson's Bay.

1638. W. J. Blaeu's *Atlas*.

1639. Kupiloff crosses Siberia to the east coast.

1642. Abel Jansen Tasman discovers Van Diemen's Land (Tasmania) and Staaten Land (New Zealand).

1642. Wasilei Pojarkof traces the course of the Amur.

1643. Hendrik Brouwer identifies New Zealand.

1643. Tasman discovers Fiji.

1645. Michael Staduchin reaches the Kolima.

1645. Nicolas Sanson's atlas.

1645. Italian Capuchin Mission explores the lower Congo.

1648. The Cossack Dishinef sails between Asia and America.

1650. Staduchin reaches the Anadir, and meets Dishinef.

1682. La Salle descends the Mississippi.

1696. Russians reach Kamtschatka.

1699. Dampier discovers his strait.

1700. Delisle's maps.

1701. Sinpopoff describes the land of the Tschutkis.

1718. Jesuit map of China and East Asia published by the Emperor Kang-hi.

1721. Hans Egédé re-settles Greenland.

1731. Hadley invented the sextant.

1731. Krupishef sails round Kamtschatka.

1731. Paulutski travels round the north-east corner of

Siberia.

1735-37. Maupertuis measures an arc of the meridian.

1739-44. Lord George Anson circumnavigates the globe.

1740. Varenne de la Véranderye discovers the Rocky Mountains.

1741. Behring discovers his strait.

1742. Chelyuskin discovers his cape.

1743-44. La Condamine explores the Amazon.

1745-61. Bourguignon d'Anville produces his maps.

1761-67. Carsten Niebuhr surveys Arabia.

1764. John Byron surveys the Falkland Islands.

1765. Harrison perfects the chronometer.

1767. First appearance of the *Nautical Almanac.*

1768. Carteret discovers Pitcairn Island, and sails through St. George's Channel, between New Britain and New Ireland.

1768-71. Cook's first voyage; discovers New Zealand and east coast of Australia; passes through Torres Strait.

1769-71. Hearne traces river Coppermine.

1769-71. James Bruce re-discovers the source of the Blue Nile in Abyssinia.

1770. Liakhoff discovers the New Siberian Islands.

1771-72. Pallas surveys West and South Siberia.

1776-79. Cook's third voyage; surveys North-West Passage; discovers Owhyhee (Hawaii), where he was killed.

1785-88. La Pérouse surveys north-east coast of Asia and Japan, discovers Saghalien, and completes delimitation of the ocean.

1785-94. Billings surveys East Siberia.

1787-88. Lesseps surveys Kamtschatka and crosses the Old
World from east to west.

1788. The African Association founded.

1789-93. Mackenzie discovers his river, and first crosses
North America.

1792. Vancouver explores his island.

1793. Browne reaches Darfur, and reports the existence
of the White Nile.

1796. Mungo Park reaches the Niger.

1796. Lacerda explores Mozambique.

1797. Bass discovers his strait.

1799-1804. Alexander von Humboldt explores South
America.

1800-4. Lewis and Clarke explore the basin of the
Missouri.

1801-4. Flinders coasts south coast of Australia.

1805-7. Pike explores the country between the sources of
the Mississippi and the Red River.

1810-29. Malte-Brun publishes his *Géographic Universelle*.

1814. Evans discovers Lachlan and Macquarie rivers.

1816. Captain Smith discovers South Shetland Isles.

1817-20. Spix and Martius explore Brazil.

1817. First edition of Stieler's atlas.

1817-22. Captain King maps the coast-line of Australia.

1819-22. Franklin, Back, and Richardson attempt the
North-West Passage by land.

1819. Parry discovers Lancaster Strait and reaches 114°
W.

1820-23. Wrangel discovers his land.

1821. Bellinghausen discovers Peter Island, the most

southerly land then known.

1822. Denham and Clapperton discover Lake Tchad, and visit Sokoto.

1822-23. Scoresby explores the coast of East Greenland.

1823. Weddell reaches 74.15° S.

1826. Major Laing is murdered at Timbuctoo.

1827. Parry reaches 82.45° N.

1827. Réné Caillié visits Timbuctoo.

1828-31. Captain Sturt traces the Darling and the Murray.

1829-33. Ross attempts the North-West Passage; discovers Boothia Felix.

1830. Royal Geographical Society founded, and next year united with the African Association.

1831-35. Schomburgk explores Guiana.

1831. Captain Biscoe discovers Enderby Land.

1833. Back discovers Great Fish River.

1835-49. Junghuhn explores Java.

1837. T. Simpson coasts along the north mainland of North America 1277 miles.

1838-40. Wood explores the sources of the Oxus.

1838-40. Dumont d'Urvilie discovers Louis-Philippe Land and Adélie Land.

1839. Balleny discovers his island.

1839. Count Strzelecki discovers Gipps' Land.

1840. Captain Sturt travels in Central Australia.

1840-42. James Ross reaches 78.10° S.; discovers Victoria Land, and the volcanoes Erebus and Terror.

1841. Eyre traverses south of Western Australia.

1842-62. E. F. Jomard's *Monuments de la Géographie*

published.

1843-47. Count Castelnau traces the source of the Paraguay.

1844. Leichhardt explores Southern Australia.

1845. Huc explores Tibet.

1845. Petermann's *Mittheilungen* first published.

1845-47. Franklin's last voyage.

1846. First edition of K. v. Spruner's *Historische Handatlas*.

1847. J. Rae connects Hudson's Bay with east coast of Boothia.

1848. Leichhardt attempts to traverse Australia, and disappears.

1849-56. Livingstone traces the Zambesi and crosses South Africa.

1850-54. M'Clure succeeds in the North-West Passage.

1850-55. Barth explores the Soudan.

1853. Dr. Kane explores Smith's Sound.

1854. Rae hears news of the Franklin expedition from the Eskimo.

1854-65. Faidherbe explores Senegambia.

1856-57. The brothers Schlagintweit cross the Himalayas, Tibet, and Kuen Lun.

1856-59. Du Chaillu travels in Central Africa.

1857-59. M'Clintock discovers remains of the Franklin expedition, and explores King William Land.

1858. Burton and Speke discover Lake Tanganyika, and Speke sees Lake Victoria Nyanza.

1858-64. Livingstone traces Lake Nyassa.

1859. Valikhanoft reaches Kashgar.

1860. Burke travels from Victoria to Carpentaria.

1860. Grant and Speke, returning from Lake Victoria Nyanza, meet Baker coming up the Nile.

1861-62. M'Douall Stuart traverses Australia from south to north.

1863. W. G. Palgrave explores Central and Eastern Arabia.

1864. Baker discovers Lake Albert Nyanza.

1868. Nordenskiold reaches his highest point in Greenland, 81.42°.

1868-71. Ney Elias traverses Mid-China.

1868-74. John Forrest penetrates from Western to Central Australia.

1869-71. Schweinfurth explores the Southern Soudan.

1869-74. Nachtigall explores east of Tchad.

1870. Fedchenko discovers Transalai, north of Pamir.

1870. Douglas Forsyth reaches Yarkand.

1871-88. The four explorations of Western China by Prjevalsky.

1872-73. Payer and Weiprecht discover Franz Josef Land.

1872-76. H.M.S. *Challenger* examines the bed of the ocean.

1872-76. Ernest Giles traverses North-West Australia.

1873. Colonel Warburton traverses Australia from east to west.

1873. Livingstone discovers Lake Moero.

1874-75. Lieut. Cameron crosses equatorial Africa.

1875-94. Élisée Reclus publishes his *Géographie Universelle*.

1876. Albert Markham reaches 83.20° N. on the Nares expedition.

1876-77. Stanley traces the course of the Congo.

1878-82. The Pundit Krishna traces the course of the Yangtse, Pekong, and Brahmaputra.

1878-79. Nordenskiold solves the North-East Passage along the north coast of Siberia.

1878-84. Joseph Thomson explores East-Central Africa.

1878-85. Serpa Pinto twice crosses Africa.

1879-82. The *Jeannette* passes through Behring Strait to the mouth of the Lena.

1880. Leigh Smith surveys south coast of Franz Josef Land.

1880-82. Bonvalot traverses the Pamirs.

1881-87. Wissmann twice crosses Africa, and discovers the left affluents of the Congo.

1883. Lockwood, on the Greely Mission, reaches 83.23° N., north cape of Greenland.

1886. Francis Garnier explores the course of the Mekong.

1887. Younghusband travels from Pekin to Kashmir.

1887-89. Stanley conducts the Emin Pasha Relief Expedition across Africa, and discovers the Pigmies, and the Mountains of the Moon.

1888. F. Nansen crosses Greenland from east to west.

1888-89. Captain Binger traces the bend of the Niger.

1889. The brothers Grjmailo explore Chinese Turkestan.

1889-90. Bonvalot and Prince Henri d'Orléans traverse Tibet.

1890. Selous and Jameson explore Mashonaland.

1890. Sir W. Macgregor crosses New Guinea.

1891-92. Monteil crosses from Senegal to Tripoli.

1892. Peary proves Greenland an island.

1893. Mr. and Mrs. Littledale travel across Central Asia.

1893-97. Dr. Sven Hedin explores Chinese Turkestan, Tibet, and Mongolia.

1893-97. Dr. Nansen is carried across the Arctic Ocean in the *Fram*, and advances farthest north (86.14° N.).

1894-95. C. E. Borchgrevink visits Antarctica.

1894-96. Jackson-Harmsworth expedition in Arctic lands.

1896. Captain Bottego explores Somaliland.

1896. Donaldson Smith traces Lake Rudolph.

1896. Prince Henri D'Orleans travels from Tonkin to Moru.

1897. Captain Foa traverses South Africa from S. to N.

1897. D. Carnegie crosses W. Australia from S. to N.

EUROPE.

Great Britain.—B.C. 450. Himilco. *Circa* 333. Pytheas. 60-54. Cæsar.

France.—B.C. *circa* 600. Marseilles founded. 57. Cæsar.

Russia.—A.D. 1554. Richard Chancellor.

Baltic.—A.D. 890. Wulfstan and Othere.

Iceland.—A.D. 861. Naddod.

ASIA.

India.—B.C. 332. Alexander. 330. Nearchus. *Circa* 300. Megasthenes. A.D. 400-14. Fa-hien. 518-21. Hoei-Sing and Sung-Yun. 540. Cosmas Indicopleustes. 629-46. Hiouen-Tshang. 671-95. I-tsing. 1159-73. Benjamin of Tudela. 1304-78. Ibn Batuta. 1327-72. Mandeville. 1328. Jordanus of Severac. 1328-49. John de Marignolli. 1419-40. Nicolo Conti. 1442-44. Abd-ur-Razzak. 1468-74. Athanasius Nikitin. 1487. Pedro de Covilham. 1494-99. Hieronimo di Santo Stefano. 1503-8. Ludovico di Varthema.

Farther India.—A.D. 1503. Ludovico di Varthema. 1509. Lopes di Sequira. 1886. Francis Garnier.

China.—A.D. 851-916. Suláimán and Abu Zaid. 1292. John of Monte Corvino. 1316-30. Odorico di Pordenone. 1328-49. John de Marignolli. 1537-58. Ferdinand Mendez Pinto. 1868-71. Ney Elias. 1871-88. Prjevalsky.

1878-82. Pundit Krishna. 1889. Grjmailo brothers. 1896. Prince Henri d'Orléans.

Japan.—A.D. 1542. Antonio de Mota. 1785-88. La Pérouse.

Arabia.—A.D. 1761-67. Carsten Niebuhr. 1863. Palgrave.

Persia.—B.C. 332. Alexander. A.D. 1468-74. Athanasius Nikitin.

Mongolia.—A.D. 1255. Ruysbroek (Rubruquis). 1260-71. Nicolo and Maffeo Polo. 1271. Marco Polo. 1893-97. Dr. Sven Hedin.

Tibet.—A.D. 1845. Huc. 1856-7. Schlagintweit. 1878. Pundit Krishna. 1887. Younghusband. 1889-90. Bonvalot and Prince Henri d'Orléans. 1893-97. Dr. Sven Hedin.

Central Asia.—A.D. 1558. Anthony Jenkinson. 1642. Wasilei Pojarkof. 1838-40. Wood. 1859. Valikhanoff. 1870. Douglas Forsyth. 1870. Fedchenko. 1880. Bonvalot. 1893. Littledale.

Siberia.—A.D. 1579. Timovief. 1639. Kupiloff. 1644-50. Staduchin. 1648. Dshineif. 1701. Sinpopoff. 1731. Paulutski. 1742. Chelyuskin. 1771-72. Pallas. 1785-94. Billings.

Kamtschatka.—A.D. 1696. Russians. 1731. Kru pishef. 1787-88. Lesseps.

AFRICA.

A.D. *circa* 450. Hanno. 1420. Zarco. 1462. Pedro de Cintra. 1484. Diego Cam. 1486. Bartholomew Diaz. 1497. Vasco da Gama. 1520. Alvarez. 1549. Bareto and Homera. 1590. Battel. 1596. Payz. 1618. Thompson. 1623. Lobo. 1645. Italian Capuchins. 1769-71. Bruce. 1793. Browne. 1796. Mungo Park. 1796. Lacerda. 1822. Denham and Clapperton. 1826. Laing. 1827. Réné Caillié. 1849-73. Livingstone. 1850-55. Barth. 1854-65. Faidherbe. 1856-59. Du Chaillu. 1858. Burton and Speke. 1860. Grant and Speke. 1864. Baker. 1869-71. Schweinfurth. 1869-74. Nachtigall. 1874-75. Cameron. 1876-89. Stanley. 1878-84. Thomson. 1878-85. Serpa Pinto. 1881-87. Wissmann. 1888-89. Binger. 1890. Selous and Jameson. 1891-92. Monteil. 1896. Bottego. 1896. Donaldson Smith. 1897. Foa.

NORTH AMERICA.

A.D. 499. Hoei-Sin. *Circa* 1000. Lyef. 1497, 1517. John and Sebastian Cabot. 1500. Corte Real. 1513. Ponce de Leon. 1524. Verazzano. 1532. Cortez. 1534. Cartier. 1539. Ulloa. 1542. Cabrillo. 1516. Frobisher. 1586. Davis. 1592. Juan de Fuca. 1608. Champlain. 1609, 10. Hudson. 1631. Fox. 1682. La Salle. 1740. Varenne de la Véranderye 1741. Behring. 1789-93.

Mackenzie. 1792. Vancouver. 1800-4. Lewis and Clarke. 1805-7. Pike. 1837. Simpson.

SOUTH AMERICA.

A.D. 1498. Columbus. 1499-1501. Amerigo Vespucci. 1499. Pinzon. 1500. Pedro Cabral. 1517. Juan Diaz de Solis. 1519-20. Magellan. 1531. Francisco Pizarro. 1535. D'Almagro. 1536. Gonsalo Pizarro. 1541. Orellana. 1572. Juan Fernandez. 1580. Dutch in Guiana. 1615. Lemaire. 1743-44. La Condamine. 1764. John Byron. 1799-1804. Humboldt. 1817-20. Spix and Martius. 1831-35. Schomburgk. 1843-47. Castelnau.

CENTRAL AMERICA.

A.D. 1502. Columbus. 1513. Vasco Nuñez de Balbao. 1518. Grijalva. 1519. Fernando Cortez. 1519. Guray.

AUSTRALIA.

A.D. 1605. Torres. 1606. Quiros. 1616. Hartog. 1619. Edel and Houtman. 1622. The *Leeuwin.* 1627. Nuyts. 1699. Dampier. 1770. Cook. 1797. Bass. 1801-4. Flinders. 1814. Evans. 1817-22. King. 1828-40. Sturt. 1839. Strzelecki. 1841. Eyre. 1844-48. Leichhardt. 1860. Burke. 1861-62. MacDouall Stuart. 1868-74. Forrest. 1872-76. Giles. 1873. Warburton. 1897. Carnegie.

NEW ZEALAND.

A.D. 1642. Tasman. 1643. Brouwer. 1768-79. Cook.

POLYNESIA.

A.D. 1512. Francisco Serrão. 1520, 21. Magellan. 1527. Saavedra. 1542. Gaetano 1542. Ruy Lopez de Villalobos. 1543. Ortez de Retis. 1567-98. Alvaro Mendaña. 1599. Houtman. 1643. Tasman. 1768. Carteret. 1776-79. Cook. 1835-49. Junghuhn. 1890. Macgregor.

NORTH POLE.

A.D. *circa* 900. Gunbiörn. 985. Eric the Red. 1553. Willoughby. 1596. Barentz. 1603. Bennett. 1611. Jan Mayen. 1616. Baffin. 1721. Egédé. 1769-71. Hearne. 1819-22. Franklin, Back, and Richardson. 1819-27. Parry. 1820-23. Wrangel. 1822-23. Scoresby. 1829-33. Ross. 1833. Back. 1845-47. Franklin. 1847-54. Rae. 1850-54. M'Clure. 1853. Kane. 1857-59. M'Clintock. 1868-79. Nordenskiöld. 1872-73. Payer and Weiprecht. 1876. Markham. 1879-82. The *Jeannette.* 1880. Leigh Smith. 1883. Lockwood. 1888-97. Nansen. 1892. Peary. 1894-96. Jackson-Harmsworth expedition.

SOUTH POLE.

A.D. 1816. Capt. Smith. 1821. Bellinghausen. 1823. Weddell. 1831. Biscoe. 1838-40. Dumont d'Urville. 1839. Balleny. 1840-42. James Ross. 1894-95. Borchgrevink.

CIRCUMNAVIGATORS.

A.D. 1522. Sebastian del Cano. 1577-79. Drake. 1739-44. Lord George Anson.

ATLANTIC OCEAN.

A.D. 1400. Jehan Bethencourt. 1432. Cabral. 1442. Nuño Tristão. 1471. Pedro d'Escobar. 1471. Fernando Po. 1492-93. Columbus. 1501. Juan di Nova. 1501. Tristan d'Acunha. 1502. Bermudez.

INDIAN OCEAN.

A.D. 1505. Mascarenhas.

PROGRESS OF GEOGRAPHICAL SCIENCE.

B.C. 570. Anaximander of Miletus. 501. Hecatæus of Miletus. 446. Herodotus. *Circa* 200. Eratosthenes. 100. Marinus of Tyre. 20. Strabo. Before 12. Agrippa. A.D. 150. Ptolemy. 230. Peutinger Table. 776. Beatus. 884. Ibn Khordadbeh. 912-30. Mas'udi. 921. Ahmed Ibn Fozlan. 969. Ibn Haukal. 1111. Water-compass. 1154. Edrisi. *Circa* 1180. Alexander Neckam. 1280. Hereford map. 1284. Ebstorf map. 1290. The normal Portulano. 1320. Flavio Gioja. 1339. Dulcert. 1351. Medicean Portulano. 1375. Cresquez. 1419. Prince Henry the Navigator. 1457. Fra Mauro. 1474. Toscanelli. 1478. 2nd ed. Ptolemy. 1492. Behaim. 1500. Juan de la Cosa. 1507-13. Waldseemüller. 1520. Schoner. 1538. Mercator. 1544. Munster. 1556-72. Laperis. 1573. Ortelius. 1592. Molyneux globe. 1598. Hakluyt. 1630. Ferro meridian fixed. 1638. Blaeu. 1645. Sanson. 1700. Delisle. 1718. Jesuit map of China. 1731. Hadley. 1735-37. Maupertuis. 1745-61. Bourguiguon d'Anville. 1765. Harrison. 1767. Nautical Almanac. 1788. African Association. 1810-29. Malte-Brun. 1817. Stieler. 1830. Royal Geographical Society founded. 1842. Jomard 1845. Petermann. 1846. Spruner. 1875-94. Élisée Reclus. 1872-76. The *Challenger*.

Milton Keynes UK
Ingram Content Group UK Ltd.
UKHW030838021124
450589UK00006B/689

9 789362 925039